**Walking Eye**
mobile app

Discover the world's best destinations with the Insight Guides Walking Eye app, available to download for free in the App Store and Google Play.

The container app provides easy access to fantastic free content on events and activities taking place in your current location or chosen destination, with the possibility of booking, as well as the regularly-updated Insight Guides travel blog: Inspire Me. In addition, you can purchase curated, premium destination guides through the app, which feature local highlights, hotel, bar, restaurant and shopping listings, an A to Z of practical information and more. Or purchase and download Insight Guides eBooks straight to your device.

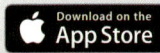 

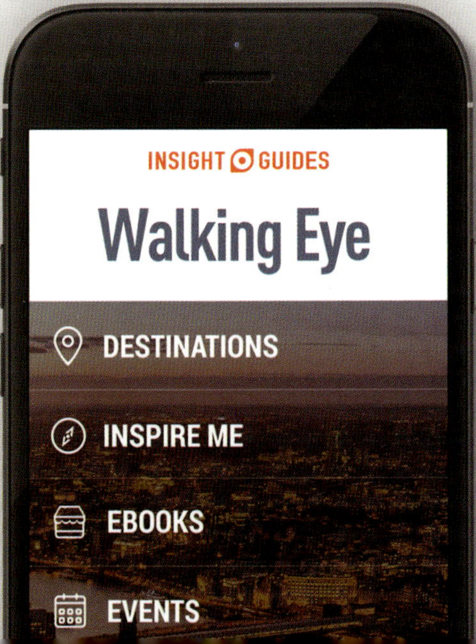

TOP 10 ATTRACTIONS

CARTAGENA'S WALLED CITY
Walk along the ancient ramparts of this fortress city and feel the might once wielded by colonial Spain. See page 49.

ZONA CAFETERA
South of Manizales lies Colombia's premier coffee-growing region. See page 43.

CIUDAD PERDIDA
Not all ancient cities in South America are in Peru: these ruins pre-date Machu Picchu by 650 years. See page 58.

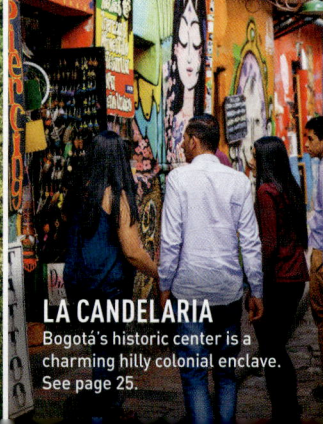

LA CANDELARIA
Bogotá's historic center is a charming hilly colonial enclave. See page 25.

MONSERRATE
Some of the greatest panoramic views in South America can be seen at Cristo Redentor, Machu Picchu – and Cerro Monserrate. See page 28.

SAN GIL
Home of Colombia's adventure-sports scene. See page 38.

GUAJIRA PENINSULA
Colombia's largest indigenous community live in this coastal area. See page 59.

CHOCÓ
Visit the Chocó Department for the amazing wildlife, like the annual migration of humpback whales. See page 75.

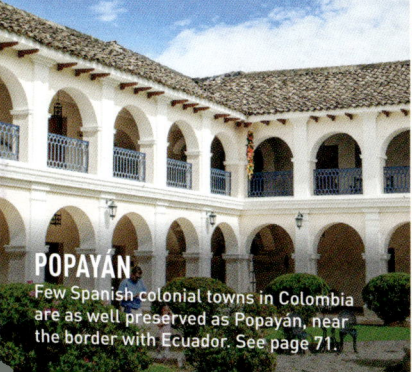

POPAYÁN
Few Spanish colonial towns in Colombia are as well preserved as Popayán, near the border with Ecuador. See page 71.

CAÑO CRISTALES
Declared off limits in 1989, Caño Cristales is open for business again. See page 81.

A PERFECT DAY

`8.00am`

Breakfast in Bogotá
Start the day the Colombian way, with a hearty breakfast. Head to Avenida Jimenez and the border between the city center and La Candelaria historic district. Here you'll find plenty of cafeterias serving Andean cold-weather breakfast staples. Try the *huevos rancheros* (eggs scrambled with tomatoes and onions) served with a warming cup of hot chocolate.

`11.00am`

Take a City Tour
Now it's time to see the city in a different way. One popular option is to take a bicycle or walking tour of Bogotá. Most tours leave from La Candelaria and, depending whether you're traveling on wheels or by foot, cover at least the historic center and often north to other places like Simón Bolívar Park and the newly trendy neighborhood of El Chapinero.

`1.00pm`

Lunch in the Historic Center
By now, you've surely worked up an appetite. Head to the historic Plaza Bolívar, which is the expansive seat of government in Colombia. After a spot of lunch, take a look around La Catedral and the grand colonial-era Roman Catholic church, then head to the northwest corner where it meets Calle 11.

`9.00am`

Visit the Museums
Bogotá is home to the famous Museo del Oro (the Gold Museum). Located at Carerra Six (in the Banco de la Republicá building), the Museo del Oro holds the most comprehensive collection of Pre-Columbian gold (some 55,000 pieces) artifacts in Latin America.

IN BOGOTÁ

4.00pm

Cerro Monserrate
Head back west, past La Candelaria and into the hills overlooking the city. Here you'll find Cerro Monserrate, a 3,152-meter (10,340ft) hill atop which sits a grand lookout featuring restaurants, an outdoor market, and a whitewashed colonial church. Take the *teleferico* (cable car) up to the summit, or walk up via the footpath.

10.00pm

A Night Out in the Zona Rosa
No visit to Colombia's capital is complete without a late night bar hop. There are plenty of neighborhoods in which to enjoy a good pub crawl, but most travelers head to the Zona Rosa (or Zona T). This T-shaped intersection of streets, north of the Zona G, packs many, many bars and clubs into a small area.

2.00pm

Mercado Paloquemao
Now it's time to visit the source of Bogotá's culinary culture. Take a bus or taxi east from Calle 19 from downtown to Carerra 22, where at the corner you'll find the Mercado Paloquemao. This municipal market takes up an entire city block and is a labyrinth of fresh fruits stalls, fishmongers, and butcher shops.

7.00pm

Dinner in the Zona G
At the edge of the Chapinero neighborhood, in the north of Bogotá, you'll find an area known as the "gourmet zone", or Zona G. The Zona G is packed full of some of the most eclectic eateries in the city. Make this your dinner stop; within just a few city blocks you can travel around the culinary world.

CONTENTS

- **INTRODUCTION** 10
- **A BRIEF HISTORY** 15
- **WHERE TO GO** 25

Bogotá 25
La Candelaria 25, Plaza Bolivar 26, The Gold Museum 27,
Monserrate 28, El Chapinero 29, Zona Rosa 29

Around Bogotá 30
Villa de Leyva 30, Zipaquirá and the Salt Cathedral 30

Antioquia 31
Medellín 32, Guatapé and El Peñol 34, Santa Fe de Antioquia 35,
Jardín 36, Reserva Natural Cañon del Río Claro 37

Santander 37
San Gil 38, Barichara 40, Bucaramanga 41, Cúcuta 42

Zona Cafetera 43
Manizales 44, Parque Ecológico Río Blanco 45, Pereira 46,
Salento 46, Parque Nacional Los Nevados 47

Cartagena 48
Walking the ramparts 48, Getsemaní 49, The walled city 49,
Bocagrande 51, Isla Tierrabomba and Isla de Barú 52

Caribbean Coast 53
Barranquilla 53, Santa Marta 54, Rodadero 56, Taganga 57,
Parque Nacional Tayrona 57, Ciudad Perdida and El Pueblito 58

Guajira — 59
Riohacha 59, Palomino 60, Santuario Los Flamencos 60, Uribía 61, Cabo de la Vela 62, Punta Gallinas 62, Parque Nacional Natural Macuira 63, Maicao 64

San Andrés Island — 65
Providencia 68

Cali — 68
San Antonio and the West 70, The North and East 71

South of Cali — 71
Popayán 72, Tierradentro 74, Pasto and the Far South 74, Ipiales 75

Chocó — 75
Quibdó 78, Nuquí 79, Parque Nacional Natural Utría 79, El Valle 80, Bahía Solano 80

Los Llanos and the Amazonas — 80
Isla de los Micos 84, Puerto Nariño 84

WHAT TO DO — 87

The Arts — 89
Adventure Sports — 92
Children's Colombia — 95

EATING OUT — 98

A-Z TRAVEL TIPS — 114

RECOMMENDED HOTELS — 134

DICTIONARY — 141

INDEX — 165

INTRODUCTION

Colombia is a land of contradictions and consistency, harmony and discord. On the one hand it's renowned for its natural beauty and rich history steeped in indigenous culture. On the other hand, it's a country that's been embroiled in civil war for over half a century, and this legacy of violence often stalks Colombia's reputation. But today a new dawn rises over the nation's Andean highlands, its Caribbean beaches, its virgin rainforests, and all the natural beauty that has made Colombia a favorite with travelers from all over the world.

CONSIDER THE CONTRADICTIONS

The country's population of nearly 50 million people is sizeable, but you'd never know it as you journey along the rolling green hills of the Antioquia region, or the fertile Cauca Valley, or the parched deserts of Guajira. There are places in Colombia that seem lost in time – like the Chocó region of the Pacific coast, where the songs of migrating humpback whales carry through the air and mix with the Afro-Caribbean drums sounded by locals in the throes of their annual music festivals.

In the south, the Amazon rainforest is a remote and unspoiled eco-wonderland whose blanket of electric green jungle canopy conceals a universe of exotic flora and fauna. The scarlet macaw, poison dart frog, and the world's tiniest primate – the pygmy marmoset – call this region home. Hear the calls of these creatures as you travel up that most primal of arterial waterways: the Amazon River. Here you can also expect to find frolicking pink river dolphins, stoic caimans, and slithering anacondas. And throughout the region indigenous locals still live simply, in harmony with their surroundings, much the way they did hundreds of years ago before any Spanish conquistador put his buckled boot on Colombian soil.

Woman at the Wayúu Cultural Festival

Contrast this with the Colombia of the 21st century: the capital of Bogotá is a dense metropolis – a ball of kinetic energy, always moving, pulling you in a hundred directions at once. At one end of the city, in the upscale Zona Rosa district, modern shopping complexes abound with affluent patrons and nightclubs pulse until the early hours. At the other end, Bogotá's cobbled streets and sprawling plazas are testament to Spain's colonization. Yet one constant remains: in Bogotá, as you'll find throughout this unforgettable country, untouched beauty exists side by side with heart-breaking poverty.

In every corner of Colombia, people struggle to get by. But the hard realities of daily toil haven't dulled Colombians' indefatigable spirit, their natural warmth, or their exuberant personality. They love people and music, dance and parties; they welcome visitors from all walks of life with open arms, ready to show off the beauty of their homeland. It's this spirit of conviviality that is the reason why Colombia is consistently ranked as one of the happiest countries in the world.

There's a lot to show off, too. Geographically, Colombia is the only country in South America possessing both a Caribbean and Pacific coast. There's literally something for everyone here. Fancy an island hop? You can bounce between the azure waters and white-sand beaches of Isa San Andrés before jetting off to nearby Providencia and diving its coral reef. Maybe embark on a desert adventure across the Guajira Peninsula, where you'll find the northernmost point on the South American continent. Then there's all those jungles and rainforests, from Tayrona National Park on the Caribbean coast all the way south to the Amazon and the borders with Brazil and Peru.

Throughout it all you'll find indigenous culture. Tayrona Park, in fact, is home to the Kogi people, direct descendants of the Tairona tribe. It was the Tairona people who built some of the ancient sites that are still standing in this tropical protected area. One such landmark is Ciudad Perdida (the Lost City), a remote grouping of indigenous ruins that rival Machu Picchu for spectacle.

Unfortunately, this peaceful existence wasn't destined to last. The Spaniards first arrived here at the turn of the 16th century, blinded by visions of wealth and dreams of El Dorado, a mythical lost city of gold. They never found El Dorado, but they plundered enough gold from the indigenous to create 100 El Dorados. That legacy is seen in the plazas of Santa Marta – the founding site of the country – and written on the ancient ramparts of fortress cities like Cartagena.

It is the coast, and Cartagena in particular, that became the starting point for a confluence of races

The home of salsa

If you want to get to the beating heart of Colombia, look no further than salsa. From Cartagena to Medellín, from Barranquilla to Bogotá, sultry syncopations blaze a trail through the country, with all roads leading to one place: Cali, the salsa capital of Colombia. Everyone here dances it, young and old, male or female. This music has helped many Colombians through some of the nation's darkest times.

and peoples who would end up defining Colombia. The Spaniards came for gold, and brought slaves who introduced their Afro-Caribbean culture that is so prevalent in coastal Colombia today. You can still see remnants of this culture on the streets in Cartagena and in the the *palenqueras*, women in traditional dress and headscarves who balance bowls of fruit on their heads in the hopes of snagging a few pesos from tourists.

Salsa show in Cali

You also hear it in the music. The Afro-Caribbean population mingled with immigrants from Europe over the years, and this created much of the music that is the lifeblood of Colombian culture to this very day: *cumbia* and *vallenato* are both genres that are as distinct as they are varied, yet unmistakably Colombian. All of this musical heritage mixed together and evolved, leading inexorably to the rise of the musical form that overtook the country and came to define it: salsa.

Unfortunately, for too many years that music and Colombia's rich culture was drowned out by the country's tragic history. For decades the Colombia was notorious for internecine strife and larger-than-life *narcotraficantes* – drug traffickers, or "narcos". Men like Pablo Escobar and the Rodríguez Orejuela brothers ruled their cocaine empires with an iron fist. On the other end of the spectrum, left-wing guerrillas waged a seemingly endless

Traditionally dressed man in Jardín

war against the government. For many years, Colombia was known more for assassinations and bombings than eco-tourism and adventure.

But something happened on the way to Colombia becoming a failed state. The people took back their country from the forces that threatened to destroy it, and took pride in their nation once again. Literary lion Gabriel García Márquez revealed the wild, magical dream of Colombia to the world, and for that he was awarded the Nobel Prize. Interest began to percolate, and when tourism spiked in the mid-2000s the message was clear: Colombia is open for business once again.

Today, the narcos are no more. The left-wing guerrillas, right-wing paramilitaries, and national government are moving inexorably (although obliquely) towards a ceasefire. The promise of total peace is within touching distance, and the world is taking notice. To the travelers and tourists who now descend upon Colombia year after year, it's a place where life becomes a dream and reality becomes magic. To many locals, Colombia is paradise lost – and found once again. It's an unfinished work of art, ever-evolving, sometimes tortured, occasionally tragic, but always worth fighting for. Even amid its often harsh realities and glaring economic iniquity, there's little that can temper the vivid magic of Colombia's beautiful dream.

A BRIEF HISTORY

Colombia wears its history on its sleeve. Well-preserved archeological sites exist throughout the country, and the cultures of its indigenous peoples are part of the national fabric. This makes it easier to gain an insight into the earliest inhabitants of the region. Some archeologists believe that the first people arrived in Colombia around 45,000 BC, but most estimates place the timeline closer to 16,000 BC.

FROM HUNTER-GATHERERS TO SOCIETIES

The first people arrived in Colombia during the Late Pleistocene era. The archeological sites in Tibitó (located in the Andean plateaus north of Bogotá), El Totumo (in the Magadalena Valley), and Cudinamarca are generally regarded as the earliest sites of human occupation in the country. To put that into perspective, when these early humans appeared, mastodons still roamed the land and were a principal source of food.

Between 5000 and 1000 BC these hunter-gatherers shifted to an agrarian society, establishing permanent settlements. By the first millennium, the tribes developed sophisticated political systems and social organizations. The Tairona, for example, who existed in the coastal Sierra Nevadas, were one of the most advanced of the early societies. Other indigenous tribes include the Muisca, who controlled the central Colombian highlands and whose first settlements date back to around 545 BC. Today there are 102 indigenous groups in Colombia. Some still live in tribes to this day, existing much the same as they did before Europeans arrived with fever dreams of gold.

HISTORY

THE SPANISH ARRIVE

The Spanish colonization of present-day Colombia was a gradual process. The first European to arrive was a Spanish explorer named Alonso de Ojeda. He spent a brief period on Colombia's Caribbean coast, and when he returned to Spain he brought with him stories of limitless reserves of native gold, which helped give rise to the famous El Dorado legend.

In 1533 the Spanish commander Pedro de Heredia founded what is now the city of Cartagena. It was conceived as a fortress city, safe from pirate attacks, where the Spanish could stockpile massive amounts of gold. It grew rapidly as the Spanish acquired more treasure, much of it plundered form the tombs of the Sinú indigenous tribes. Also, during the early decades of the 16th century, Europeans began bringing the first enslaved Africans to Colombia. Cartagena thus became the chief slave port in the country.

Humble beginnings

Around 1500, Rodrigo de Bastidas, a conquistador with a reputation for insubordination, arrived on the Colombian Caribbean coast. He established the present-day city of Santa Marta, named because it was founded on the day of St Martha's Feast. This was the first permanent settlement in Colombia, and was officially founded in 1525. It's the oldest remaining city in Colombia.

Spain's hunger for gold led to their conquest of the two main indigenous groups: the Tairona and Muisca tribes. In 1535, a conquistador named Gonzalo Jiménez de Quesada led an expedition of 800 men south from Santa Marta into the Andes region around modern-day Bogotá – the heart of the Muisca nation. In 1537 the natives mounted a spirited resistance; however, Quesada's expedition dominated through sheer military might. Quesada officially founded Santa Fé de Bogotá in 1538.

The Spanish then struck out into the central Andean plains and destroyed the Muisca hierarchy. The remaining natives were allotted parcels of land, but they were forced to work it for the conquerors. This was a profitable labor system the Spanish implemented in various regions of the Americas. It was known as *ecomienda*, which is a colloquial way of saying 'slave labor.'

Alonso De Ojeda and his men battling Colombian natives

INDEPENDENCE FROM SPAIN

The Spaniards had a good run in Colombia, accumulating plenty of wealth and territory, but it was about to come to an end. Revolutionary stirrings began to take hold in the public consciousness. This was due in large part to education. As more and more people were educated in the country, resentment simmered among lower classes toward the wealthy and entitled Spanish aristocracy.

On July 20, 1810, the inhabitants of Bogotá revolted and overthrew the Spanish. Around this time a young, charismatic, European-educated revolutionary was making noise in Venezuela. Simón Bolívar (1783–1830) was a Venezuelan creole (Spanish American) by birth but he would go on to lead armies of pro-independence patriots. In fact, Some 50 years before President of

Bust of Simon Bolívar

the United States Abraham Lincoln drafted his famous proclamation, Bolívar issued emancipation to all slaves willing to fight for liberation and independence.

Over the years there were a number of reversals, with Bolívar taking control of the Magdalena River and Venezuela, before Venezuelan leaders retook the land. However, in 1819 Bolívar led a force of about 2,500 men in a perilous journey over the Andes to mount their attack. They surprised the Spanish in July of 1819 near Bogotá, issuing the final blow at the Battle of Boyacá. Later that year Bolívar assumed the Presidency of Gran Colombia, the name given to the new union of countries, which included Colombia, Venezuela, Ecuador, and Panama.

It was in present-day Ciudad Bolívar, in Venezuela, that La Republica de Gran Colombia was established on December 17 1819. In 1821 a constitution was drafted with Bolívar succeeding in codifying centralization into the document, officially dividing Colombia into 26 provinces within 12 departments. The slave trade was abolished, as was the Inquisition, and lands were redistributed to the indigenous.

By 1828, amid political infighting, Bolívar's grand vision of a united Latin America was starting to fall apart. The Liberator was forced out of government and died in exile in Santa Marta in 1830, the same year that Venezuela and Ecuador broke away from the government. The hacienda where Bolívar passed away, the Quinta de San Pedro Alejandrino, still exists and is now a museum.

In 1886 the nation adopted the name it is known by today: The Republic of Colombia.

COLOMBIA IN MODERN TIMES

The 20th century saw Colombia descend into one of its darkest chapters of prolonged violence. To understand how the culture of violence first took hold, it's necessary to understand the legacy of internecine strife within the nation. Almost from the moment the constitution was drafted in 1821, rival political factions fought over the direction of the country. These opposing forces evolved over the 19th century to become two parties: pro-clerical conservatives in favor of a centralized government, and anti-clerical liberals in favor of state autonomy.

This internal strife led to *La Violencia*, Colombia's bloodiest civil war. It was fought in the 1940s and 50s principally between the conservative and liberal political parties, but many of the fighters and victims were *campesinos*, poor people who lived and toiled in the country, far away from the halls of power in Bogotá. The Violence, as the name translates to in English, was a chillingly apt name for the conflict – over the course of a decade some 200,000 people were killed.

After 10 years of civil war, proxy war, rioting, internal strife, millions of displaced citizens, lack of civil authority, media blackouts, and the occasional military coup, the two major political parties decided enough was enough. In July 1957 the former conservative and liberal Presidents Laureano Gómez and Alberto Lleras declared a *Frente Nacional* (National Front), or a joint-government comprised equally of conservatives and liberals.

The forming of the National Front ended the civil war and ushered in an era of tenuous cooperation. Liberal presidents instituted agrarian reforms, while conservative presidents expanded upon these land entitlements. For a time it seemed like the country could function, until the Conservative Party gained more power than the liberals, and outside opposition threatened to upend the entire agreement. This came in the form of communism.

In the period after World War II through to the 1960s, communism had taken root in certain areas of the country. The *Partido Comunista Colombiano*, or PPC (the Colombian Communist Party), had fostered popular fronts in urban regions as well as indoctrinated peasants in rural areas with the stated goal of improving education and working conditions. Protests and strikes were many, and land seizures were common.

On April 19th, 1970, a PCC organizer named Pedro Antonio Marín, better known as Manuel Marulanda Vélez, lost in the presidential election to Conservative Party candidate Misael Pastrana. Supporters of Vélez accused the conservatives of rigging the election and rose up to form one of Colombia's most famous guerrilla organizations: *Movimiento 19 de Abril*, or M19. These guerrilla groups, along with others like the National Liberation Army (ELN) and the *Fuerzas Armadas Revolucionarias de Colombia* (the Revolutionary Armed Forces of Colombia), known more commonly as FARC, pressed forward for years, with each claiming to represent the interests of the workers and the poor.

As if this constant warring wasn't enough, along came another other seismic shift in the Colombian landscape. During the 1970s, the global cocaine market exploded. By the mid-1970s, two dominant forces in the drug trade were established: The Medellín Cartel, famously headed by Pablo Escobar, and the Cali Cartel, formed by brothers Gilberto and Miguel Rodríguez Orejuela.

In 1982 Escobar, under the misapprehension he'd make a good politician, won a seat in Colombia's Chamber of Representatives as a liberal candidate. Unfortunately, he entered government at a time when law enforcement were first starting to openly crack down on the drug cartels. In 1984, Escobar, in a violent act of self-preservation and retaliation, had pro-extradition Justice Minister Rodrigo Lara Bonilla murdered. Escobar was seemingly invincible during this time. At the height of its power, the Medellín Cartel supplied around 80 percent of the world's cocaine, smuggling up to 15 tons into the United States each day. Consequently, Escobar made $70 million dollars profit every day, which worked out at a staggering $22 billion each year.

Pablo Escobar

However, as time wore on, and as Escobar murdered ever more police, politicians, journalists, and civilians, his downfall became inevitable. In 1985, members of M19 stormed the Colombian Supreme Court in a terrorist attack against pro-extradition judges. Half the judges on the court were executed in an event that would become known as the Siege of the Palace of Justice. The attack was allegedly backed and funded by Escobar, and marked the point where public opinion really began to turn against him.

Escobar finally met his fate on December 2nd, 1993, when an on-the-run Pablo was discovered in a safe house in Medellín.

HISTORY

He and his bodyguard tried to escape but were shot dead by the Colombian National Police, who took jubilant photos kneeling over Escobar's dead body. In 2006, the Cali Cartel brothers were extradited to Florida where they pleaded guilty to smuggling and were sentenced to 30 years each in federal prison.

With the most infamous drug traffickers dead or behind bars, Colombia turned its attention to trying to broker a peace with the country's various guerrilla groups. This would prove cumbersome; by 1990 a coalition of these guerrilla groups, which included the FARC, were operating primarily out of Antioquia and the Cauca River Valley. Despite some initial negotiation successes during the early 1990s, talks ultimately broke down in 1993 amid violent perpetrated on both sides.

Successive presidents in the 1990s tried to bring the rebels to the negotiating table, but they were often undermined by violence or political impropriety. Then, liberal President Alvaro Uribe was sworn in as president in May 2002. After many failed peace talks, few held out hope that the Harvard and Oxford-educated lawyer could successfully confront the FARC. However, Uribe did more to bring Colombia's most formidable and long-lasting rebel group to its knees than any president before him. Before he took office, the FARC controlled many urban areas. By 2010 the rebels had been pushed to the most remote corners of the country.

Since then the FARC has been on the defensive. In 2012 they entered peace talks with President Juan Manuel Santos. The Colombian people voted on a peace referendum in October 2016, narrowly rejecting it, before it was later passed by congress. The referendum never gained country-wide support, as many wounds are still raw. Half the populous isn't ready to offer concessions to rebel group members. Ultimately, no victory can be claimed until Colombia is at total peace, and Colombians finally get to live free of violence, in the country they deserve.

HISTORICAL LANDMARKS

4000 BC The first people occupy Colombia's Caribbean coast.
545 BC The Muisca tribe establishes their first settlements in Colombia.
1500 Rodrigo de Bastidas establishes the first Spanish settlement on the Caribbean coast.
1538 Gonzalo Jiménez de Quesada founds Santa Fe de Bogotá.
1819 Simón Bolivar, leader of the independence movement, wins a decisive victory over the Spanish at the Battle of Boyacá.
1830 Simón Bolívar dies in Santa Marta.
1899-1903 A Liberal revolt against the Conservative government begins *La Rebelión*, or the War of a Thousand Days, resulting in over 100,000 deaths.
1948 The socialist mayor of Bogotá, Jorge Eliécer Gaitán, is assassinated, marking the beginning of *La Violencia*, a 10-year civil war.
1964 The *Fuerzas Armadas Revolucionarias de Colombia* (FARC) forms under leader Pedro Antonio Marín, a member of the Communist Party.
1970 The *Movimiento 19 de Abril* (M19) guerrilla group, a military arm of the left-wing *Alianza Nacional Popular* (ANAPO), arises in protest at the elections.
1975 Smuggler Pablo Escobar develops his cocaine empire in Medellín.
1982 Gabriel García Márquez wins the Nobel Prize in Literature.
1985 M19 guerrillas storm the Colombian Supreme Court, resulting in the deaths of half the judges on the bench.
1989 A peace accord is signed between the government and M19, and the following year they surrender their weapons and convert into a political party named *Alianza Democratica* (M19-AD).
1993 Colombian police kill Pablo Escobar in Medellín.
1998 President Andrés Pastrana grants the FARC 42,000sq km (16,216sq miles) of land in the hope of jumpstarting the peace process. .
2012 The FARC officially enter peace talks with President Juan Manuel Santos' administration in Havana, Cuba.
2016 In a referendum, Colombians narrowly reject a peace deal between the government and the FARC, only for the government to pass it anyway.
2017 The FARC formally ends its existence as an armed group after 53 years.
2018 Iván Duque Márque, of the Democratic Center Party, elected president.

La Candelaria, Bogotá

WHERE TO GO

From the deserts of the Guajira Peninsula to the ramparts of Cartagena's walled city, to the beaches of Parque Tairona, Colombia has some of the most stunning landscapes anywhere in the world. Fly to the Chocó, on the Pacific Coast, and go whale watching, or relax in Medellín, the City of the Eternal Spring. Continue to the Amazonas and discover your inner Indiana Jones with a night-time wildlife tour, swimming with pink river dolphins, or fishing for piranha. You could spend your entire life traversing Colombia and you'd barely scratch the surface of this land of fantasy-meets-reality. So what are you waiting for?

BOGOTÁ

Despite its status as a modern capital, **Bogotá** ❶ has also retained some of the best-preserved colonial neighborhoods on the continent. The city is filled with shimmering office towers and swanky new restaurants that sit side-by-side with centuries-old churches, plazas, and homes that could have hosted Simón Bolívar for dinner in times gone by.

LA CANDELARIA

Visitors will probably want to explore the southern neighborhood of La Candelaria first, as it's easily walkable. **Parque Periodista** Ⓐ lies at the northeast end of this area, and its center statue of Simón Bolívar housed in a domed stone gazebo is unmistakable. The park is also the embarking point for many of the neighborhood's popular bicycle and graffiti tours.

BOGOTÁ

Just south of Parque Periodista lies the beginning of the colonial section of La Candelaria. Travel south into the higher streets and you'll reach the **Plaza del Chorro de Quevado** Ⓑ, at the corner of Carrera 2 and Calle 12b. This popular colonial plaza is where Bogotá is believed to have been founded in 1538.

Continue south into the hills of La Candelaria. At the top is the **Iglesia de Nuestra Señora de Egipto** Ⓒ (Church of Our Lady of Egypt; Carrera 4e, no. 10a-02; tel: 1-342 1230), a colonial church that borders the neighborhood of El Egipto, one of the poorer barrios in the city. Travel west Down Calle 11 and you'll find the **Museo Botero** Ⓓ (Calle 11, no. 41; www.banrepcultural.org/museo-botero; Wed–Sat and Mon 9am–7pm, Sun 10am–5pm, closed Tue), a must-visit museum featuring the works of one of Colombia's most famous artists, Fernando Botero. Continue down to Plaza Bolívar.

PLAZA BOLÍVAR

When you arrive in **Plaza Bolívar** Ⓔ you'll be in the colonial and historic heart of Bogotá. This sprawling square has seen a lot since it was founded in 1539. The looming and elegant **El Catedral** (Cathedral; Tue–Fri 9am–5pm, Sat–Sun 9am–6pm) sits on the plaza's northeast corner and was erected in 1823. On the west side is Bogotá's City Hall, the **Alcaldia** (Carrera 8, no. 10-65), constructed in French style, with a long arcade fronting the building. On the north, the **Palacio de Justicia** (Palace of Justice) dominates the plaza. The original building

Altitude sickness

Bogotá sits at an altitude of 2,644 meters (8,675ft) above sea level, so if you're visiting for the first time, adjust to the altitude by staying hydrated and avoiding strenuous activity for the first couple days.

was badly damaged when M19 guerrillas laid siege to it in 1985. It was rebuilt in 1999, with a focus on creating symmetry within the prized public space.

Cattycorner to the plaza, on the northeast corner of Calle 11 you'll find the **Museo de la Independencia** ❻ (Museum of Independence; Carrera 7, no. 11–28; tel: 1-334 4150; www.museoindependencia.gov.co/Paginas/english.aspx; Tue–Thu 9am–5pm, Sat–Sun 10am–4pm), also known as the Casa del Florero. It takes up two floors in an old colonial house dating back to the 16th and features interactive presentations of various periods in Colombia's history, including a harrowing retelling of the Palace of Justice Siege by M19 guerrillas.

Museo del Oro

THE GOLD MUSEUM

If you head north on Carrera 7 from Plaza Bolívar to Calle 16, you'll see **Parque Santander** ❼ On the west side of the park is the entrance to the **Museo del Oro** ❽ (Gold Museum; Carrera 6, no. 15–88; tel: 1-343 2222; www.banrepcultural.org/gold-museum/exhibition-in-bogota; Tue–Sat 9am–7pm, Sun 10am–4pm). The museum is home to over 35,000 pieces of pre-Columbian gold work and ceramics. It features, among other artifacts, *la balsa de Eldorado*, a small gold raft sculpture representative of the Muisca people's ceremonial offering to their gods.

BOGOTÁ

MONSERRATE

Head east just above La Candelaria and you'll reach the base of **Cerro Monserrate** ❶ (funicular railroad operates Tue–Fri 6.30am–11.45am, Sat 6.30am–4pm, Sun 6.30am–6.30pm; cable car operates Mon–Fri 6.30am–midnight, Sat noon–midnight, Sun 10am–4.30pm). The view from the top of this 3,152 meters (10,340ft) mountain is easily the best in the city. Capping the mountain is the white Santuario Monserrate (tel: 1-284 5700; mass times: Mon noon, Tue–Fri 10am and noon; Sat 8am, 10am, noon, and 2pm) a church built in 1915. From Monserrate's stone pathways you'll be treated to a 180-degree view of the city stretched out before you. There are two decent restaurants here as well as a tourist information kiosk.

⊘ MERCADO DE PALOQUEMAO

If you're looking for an excuse to head out west and spend some time with real Bogotános, then there's no better option than the Mercado de Paloquemao (Calle 19, no. 25-04; tel: 321-253-4290; www.plazadepaloquemao.com; Mon–Sat 4.30am–4.30pm, Sun 5am–4.30pm). This is one of great municipal markets of Latin America, and this one is big, taking up around half a city block in total. Inside, the market is just as large and labyrinthine as it appears from the outside. Narrow walkways cut through entire neighborhoods of fruit and vegetable stands, each of them selling fresh produce from local farms as well as purveyors located throughout the country. This is the best place in the city to find some of Colombia's most exotic fruits in one location, and sampling these delicious items is a must.

EL CHAPINERO

About 3km (2 miles) north of La Candelaria, along Carrera 7, is the upper-middle-class neighborhood of **El Chapinero**. This barrio is diverse in that younger generations of Colombians are moving into its stately old English-manor-style houses, and it's also home to one of the most thriving gay communities in the city. In fact, the area has an official **LGBT community center** (Calle 66, no. 9a–28; tel: 1-249 0049; www.ccdlgbt.blogspot.co.uk). Gentrification is giving the neighborhood a facelift and it may someday rival the Zona Rosa, 10 blocks to the north.

Monserrate cable car

ZONA ROSA

A quick cab ride (or brisk walk) north from El Chapinero will land you at Calle 82 and Carrera 11. This marks the beginning of Bogotá's disco and shopping district, known as the **Zona Rosa**. It's hard to miss because three giant shopping malls merge right here. The heart of the Zona Rosa is just to the north of the shopping centers, where there is a pedestrian-only throughway that forms a "T" shape – hence this district also being known as the "Zona T." Here there's a wide array of dining and drinking options including *cervecerias*, gastropubs, and Irish discos.

AROUND BOGOTÁ

Just a short distance outside Colombia's capital are a few impressive landmarks and destinations. These are worth a visit even if you only have a short time in the region. The destinations mentioned here are easily reachable by public transport or taxi from Bogotá, and there are plenty of lodging options.

VILLA DE LEYVA

Drive 3 hours north from Bogotá, and you'll arrive in the well-preserved colonial town of **Villa de Leyva** ❷. Founded in 1572, the town is in the department of Boyacá and sits at an elevation of 2,149 meters (7,000ft). The starkest example of Villa de Leyva's colonial heritage is its expansive central plaza, the **Plaza Mayor**, which is a staggering 14,000 sq meters (150,700 sq ft). There's a large colonial church fronting the plaza: the **Iglesia de Nuestra Señora del Rosario** (mass times: Mon–Fri 6pm, Sat noon and 7pm, Sun 7am, 10am, noon, and 7pm, festivals noon and 6pm). When you combine the plaza, the church, and all the colonial homes with terra-cotta roofs that make up the town, you'll see why this is a popular destination for locals and tourists alike.

ZIPAQUIRÁ AND THE SALT CATHEDRAL

Zipaquirá ❸ (colloquially known as Zipa) is a municipality in cattle-ranching country located about 45km (30 miles) north of Bogotá. It's popular with tourists because of it's the location of a rock salt mine featuring the 15th-century **Catedral de Sal** (salt cathedral; www.catedraldesal.gov.co; daily 9am–5.40pm). Early miners originally dug a shrine in the tunnel, and in 1950 they built the church. In 1954 they dedicated it to the Patron Saint of Miners, Nuestra Señora del Rosario.

The salt cathedral boasts a museum and information center, and the cost of admission includes a 75-minute guided tour. Upon entering you'll see the 14 stations of the cross, each with its own 4-meter (13ft) high cross sculpted by a different artist.

ANTIOQUIA

Salt cathedral, Zipaquirá

In central-northwestern Colombia lies a region defined by green mountain landscapes of spectacular beauty, a perfectly temperate climate, and regional culture distinct from any other place in Colombia. This land is Antioquia, and the people that inhabit it are Antioqueños, colloquially known as Paisas. The department's capital, Medellín, is an example of Paisa industriousness. Here, sleek and shiny office parks and apartment towers are connected to even the poorest neighborhoods via one of the most advanced metro systems in the world.

Yes, the drug trade in the 1980s and 90s tore through the whole of Colombia, but it was particularly cruel to Antioquia. Pablo Escobar was a natural-born Paisa, and his Medellín Cartel operated out of the city. But today the region is at relative peace, and in the last few years Antioquia is finally beginning to realize its potential and shake off the legacy of Pablo Emilio Escobar Gaviria.

Sculpture on Plaza Botero

MEDELLÍN

Nestled in the rolling green hills of Antioquia lies **Medellín** ❹, the capital of the department and a thriving contemporary city rich with unique Paisa culture. Colombians call it the "City of the Eternal Spring", and it isn't hard to see how the nickname came to be. At 1,496 meters (4,900ft) above sea level, it's located high enough in the Cordillera Central to enjoy a perpetual spring-like climate; temperatures average around 72°F (22°C) year round.

Today Medellín is a modern, thriving metropolis of about 3.8 million people that's the second-largest city in the country. It's a hotbed of art, music, commerce, and progressive thought processes. But Medellín wasn't always so vibrant and forward-thinking. At one point in the early 1990s, it was the murder capital of the world, due in no small part to Pablo Escobar's Medellín cartel wreaking havoc. But in less than three decades it has done a complete 180-degree turnaround and is now a model of social progress, revitalized by a world-class metro system and a number of civic projects.

Plaza Botero

Plaza Botero Ⓐ is the central plaza and one of the most famous in Medellín. It is located at Calle 52 and Carrera 52 and contains some 23 works donated by Colombia's most famous sculptor,

Fernando Botero. Although each is different, the sculptures all possess that unmistakable Botero style – sensual and voluptuous figures whose smooth texture is as important a part of the aesthetic as any other aspect.

The imposing Gothic building on the north side of the plaza is the **Palacio de la Cultura Rafael Uribe** (Mon–Sat 8am–noon, 2–5pm; free), which was constructed 1937. Today it's a cultural center and art gallery. Opposite is the **Museo de Antioquia** (Carrera 52, no. 52-43; tel: 4-251 3636; www.museodeantioquia.co; Mon–Sat 10am–5.30pm; contact the museum in advance to organize guided visits in English), featuring many works by Botero as well as paintings by Colombia's Francisco Antonio Cano Cardona

A block south of Plaza Botero is the **Iglesia de la Veracruz** Ⓑ (Church of the Veracruz; Carrera 51, no. 52-58). Construction of this church began in 1682 by the Spanish who settled the area and it was finally finished at the end of the 18th century. It's believed to be the oldest church in the center of the city.

Medellín's Parks

Located northeast of Plaza Botero is the **Parque Bolívar** Ⓒ, a long, stately park featuring fountains and an equestrian statue of The Liberator himself. The first Saturday of every month a craft market, the **Mercado de San Alejo** is held here. Overlooking the park from the north is the **Catedral Metropolitano**, one of the largest all-brick buildings in the world. Located three blocks south from Plaza Botero is **Parque de Berrio**, a major metro stop in the bustling heart of Medellín.

A few blocks south, on Avenida Oriental, lies **Parque San Antonio** (Calles 44/46 and Carrera 46), one of the best people-watching spots in Medellín. In its short existence the park has

ANTIOQUIA

endured tragedy: in 1995, a bomb planted by FARC went off at a concert here, killing 23 people and injuring dozens more.

The Botanical Garden

The **Joaquin Antonio Uribe Botanical Garden** D (Calle 73, no. 51d-14; tel: 4-444 5500; www.botanicomedellin.org; daily 9am-4pm; free) is a 14-hectare (34-acre) park featuring 1,000 living species of animals and some 4,500 species of plants and trees. It also has a lily-filled pond as well as various pathways leading to, among other things, the famous "Orchideorama," a 20-meter (65-ft) tall mesh canopy that protects a vital collection of orchids and a butterfly reserve.

El Poblado

South of the city center is **El Poblado** E, where Medellín first began as a humble village. Today, it is one of the trendiest, most affluent areas of the city. It's the location of **Parque Lleras**, an area commonly known as Medellín's Zona Rosa. Here you'll find a high concentration of bars, clubs, and upscale restaurants. During the day the park is filled with street artists and their paintings, and there's a nice tranquil vibe. During the evening, especially on weekends, the area gets quite touristy.

Three blocks away from Parque Lleras you'll find one of the last colonial remnants in this part of town: the **Iglesia de San José** (Church of San José; Carrera 43a, no.9-50; mass times: Mon-Sat 8am, noon, and 6.30pm; Sun 7am, 8am, 10.30am, noon, 6pm, and 7pm). The church was founded in 1616 and features an expansive pulpit and fine stained-glass mosaics

GUATAPÉ AND EL PEÑOL

When Paisas want to get away for a day trip or weekend excursion, they often come to **Guatapé** 5 located about 93km (58 miles) east of Medellín. Once you arrive you'll see why: Guatapé is adjacent to **El Peñol**, a town and its giant namesake granite rock, which juts 200 meters (650ft) out of the ground like a bullet, and is one of the major tourist attractions in Antioquia. That said most people prefer to stay in Guatapé as opposed to El Peñol because this lakeside town of about 6,000 residents is an explosion of color and activity, which is most pronounced on the *zócalos* (lower exterior portion) of the colonial houses that are found here. Even some of the mototaxis are decked out in all the colors of the visible spectrum.

El Peñol

SANTA FE DE ANTIOQUIA

Some 80km (50 miles) northwest of Bogotá, in the Cauca River Valley, is **Santa Fe de Antioquia** ❻, a medium-sized town of about 23,000 founded in 1541. Located at a lower altitude, the town enjoys a more tropical climate and is hotter than Medellín.

Immediately striking here is the colonial-style **Plaza Mayor**. The most dominant building around the plaza is a neoclassical cathedral, the **Catedral Basilica de la Inmaculada Concepción de Santa Fe** (Cathedral Basilica of the Immaculate Conception; mass times: Mon–Fri 6.45am, Sat 6.30pm, Sun 11am and 6.45pm), which was constructed between 1797 and 1837 and looks over the plaza from the west. In the plaza you'll also

Coffee shop in Jardín

find many artisan kiosks selling produce, souvenirs and handicrafts.

JARDÍN

Jardín ❼ is a small town 133km (83 miles) southwest of Medellín that is home to around 14,000 people. It is located in a valley between the western Cordillera Oriental and the San Juan River. The town itself stands out as one of the most idyllic colonial villages in the area. The central plaza, **Principle Park** (sometimes called Plaza El Libertador), is where all the action occurs. It's the location of Jardín's dominating neo-Gothic church, the **Templo Parroquial de la Inmaculada Concepción**, which is well worth a look. There's also an abundance of shopping, dining, and lodging options around the plaza.

There are two cable car lines in Jardín, which were originally meant to help connect residents from the nearby villages so they could sell their goods in town. One travels from the north of town to the top of a mountain peak called the Alto de las Flores (Flower Hilltop). It affords great views of the Jardín and there's also a restaurant there. The other line, the *garrucha*, is an older cable car that runs from the south up over a river to a hill lined with plantain trees. There's a terrace bar offering good snacks, beer, and other refreshments. The views of the town from here are stunning.

RESERVA NATURAL CAÑON DEL RÍO CLARO

One other place in Colombia where fantasy seemingly meets reality is the **Reserva Natural Cañon del Río Claro** ❽ (www.rioclaroreservanatural.com). The canyon was formed by water carving its way through the countryside on a marble riverbed, leaving sheer cliffs and hidden caves in its wake. The running waters here twist and turn their way through Antioquia, creating large pools and gulleys that act as natural bathtubs of the most vivid shades of jade.

The reserve is located 165km (103 miles) southeast of Medellín on the way to Bogotá. Río Claro is best visited over two or three days, as there are plenty of activities and sights here that are going to keep you occupied for some time. These activities include rafting, caving, swimming, and zip-lining. There are a number of lodging options at the site, ranging from rustic cabins to bungalows.

Hacienda Napoles

In a place called Puerto Triunfo, Antioquia, some 150km (93 miles) east of Medellín, is the former home of the most notorious drug lord to have ever lived, **Hacienda Napoles** ❾ (road from Medellín–Bogotá at km 165; tel: 4-444 2975; www.haciendanapoles.com; Tue–Sun 9am–5pm). Really, calling it a home is a misnomer – this was an expansive estate covering a massive 20 sq km (7.7 sq miles) of land. Pablo Escobar built Hacienda Napoles to be his prime country estate, and indeed he made it one of his principal residences. Today the home itself has fallen into disrepair, and the whole property is now a theme park complete with hotels.

SANTANDER

Head north of Bogotá, just east of the Magdalena, and when the cold and misty Andes give way to tropical cloud forest, you've arrived in Santander Department. Today the area is known for adrenaline-pumping adventure sports; in fact, Santander is the unofficial adventure sports capital of Colombia. Here you can indulge in some hair-raising feats including white-water rafting, paragliding, caving, and zip-lining.

SAN GIL

On its surface, **San Gil** ⑩ may seem like a small colonial town populated by a mere 50,000 people. However, its strategic location in the valley of the Río Fonce makes it an ideal destination for any thrill seeker. The river systems of the Fonce, Chicamora, and Suárez cut through the gorges of the surrounding Andes, facilitating some of the best rafting and kayaking in the country. Local and international travelers flock to San Gil to conquer these rivers, but they also come to trek in the lush green hills of the surrounding countryside, bathe in the natural pools and falls of the Pozo Azul, cycle through the mountains, and paraglide over the Chicamocha Canyon.

⊙ EXTREME SPORTS IN SAN GIL

Every extreme sport that Santander is famous for can be found in San Gil. Even though most high-end hotels will be happy to arrange these activities for you, it is highly recommended to go through the town hostels, like Macondo, as they have been working with local providers day-in and day-out for years. Extreme sports you can partake in here include abseiling, caving, hiking, paragliding, kayaking, rafting, mountain biking, and zip-lining.

Around town

The town's north and south sides are bisected by the Río Fonce, which runs along Carrera 11. Just south of the river and up a hill is the imposing **Central Comercial El Puente** (Calle 10, no. 12–184; tel: 7-724 4644), a huge shopping complex with a movie theater and a plethora of dining and retail options. Across the river is the **Parque Gallineral** (8am–5pm). This 4-hectare (10-acre) park is a green oasis with mini rivers running through it and featuring various species of birds and butterflies. There's a lovely natural pool here too, where weary locals come to cool off.

Rappelling down Juan Curi waterfall in San Gil

The historic heart of the town is centered around the lively **Parque Principal**. At the north end of the park is the **Catedral de la Santa Cruz** (Calle 12, no. 8–44; mass times: Mon–Sat 6am and 6.30pm, Sun 5am, 7am, 9am, 10.30am, noon, and 6.30pm), an old colonial church founded in 1791. All of the park, including the church, looks fantastic at night when it's lit up in soft colors. Here you'll also find the best nightlife in town—no bar or disco offers a better experience than having a drink with the locals who congregate on the square nightly.

Chicamocha Canyon

The **Chicamocha Canyon** ⓫ flows from Boyacá Department to Santander, where it cuts one of the deepest gorges on earth, near Bucaramanga. The result is a stunning natural phenomenon that is one of the biggest canyons in the world, and the biggest in Colombia. One of the best ways to see it on land is on the route from San Gil to Bucaramanga.

BARICHARA

In the competition among Colombia's many idyllic colonial towns as to which one reigns supreme, **Barichara** ⓬ can be found near the top. More than a few visitors have described this colonial outpost in the mountains as the most beautiful in the country—and for good reason. Here the streets are paved with hefty stones, and many of the town's oldest buildings are made of an adobe-like substance called *tapia pisada*, a type of clay. The stores and residences are almost all whitewashed, featuring terra-cotta roofs, with green trim on the doors and *zócalos* (base of the building).

Barichara is located 22km (14 miles) from San Gil, and buses make the trip frequently from San Gil (daily every 30 minutes from 6am to 8pm), dropping you off in the Parque Principal.

Exploring Barichara

This town is small enough (population around 10,000) that you can get around entirely on foot, as long as you're prepared to hike up some hills. It's best to use the main park—the **Parque Principal**—as your main point of reference. Many of the best hostels and hotels are located just a block or two from here, as are the best restaurants and cafés. The park itself is small but ideal, with a central stone water fountain where local children come to beat the heat.

On the northwest side of the park is the **Catedral de la Inmaculada Concepción** (Church of the Immaculate Conception; mass times: Tue–Sat 6am and 6pm, Sun 5am, 10am, noon, and 6pm), a great sandstone church with twin bell towers. For the best views, head to the north end of town and to the **observation point**. Here you'll be treated to panoramic views of the valley of the Río Suarez. There are also great views of the surrounding mountains up the road at the **Jardín**, which is just behind the Capilla Santa Barbara. This pleasant little park features a small stone amphitheater, which hosts free live music concerts and events once every couple of months or so.

BUCARAMANGA

Roughly 420km (260 miles) from Bogotá is the city of **Bucaramanga** ⓭. If you're traveling north from San Gil, passing through the Chicamocha Canyon, the sight of a giant modern metropolis appearing seemingly out of nowhere may well throw you. Industry is responsible for all this growth; this city of around 600,000 has boomed due in no small part to the success of Colombian coffee and tobacco on the international market. Some of Colombia's best paragliding spots are just outside town.

Exploring Bucamaranga

There are a few areas in the city worth looking around, and one of them is the historic center. The palm-lined **Parque García Rovira** is the epicenter of this part of town. Here you will find many cultural centers and museums,

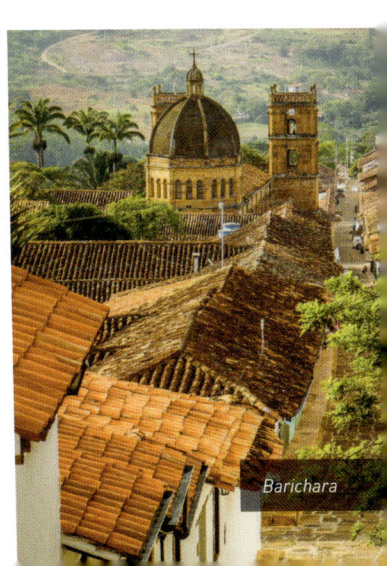

Barichara

including the **Casa de Bolívar** (Calle 37, no. 12–15; tel: 7-630 4258; Mon–Sat 8am–noon, 2–6pm), a colonial home where Simon Bolívar once lived when he made this then-village his base of operations in 1813. On the east side of the park is the **Iglesia San Laureano** (Carrera 12, no. 36–08), which was rebuilt in 1872 on the site of a 1778 church.

Parque Santander is the heart of the modern center of the city, and it is where many budget hotels can be found. This is the location of one of the most famous churches in Bucaramanga, the **Catedral de la Sagrada Familia** (Calle 36, no. 19–56; Mon 8am–noon, 1–3pm, Sun 8am–1pm). There is also the **Parque San Pio** (Carrera 5, no. 33), which is surrounded by nice restaurants as well as the **Iglesia San Pio**, a Modernist church featuring works by Oscar Rodríguez Naranjo, another Santandereano. The **Museo de Arte Moderno** (Calle 37, no. 26–16; tel: 7- 645 0483; Mon–Fri 8am–noon and 2–6pm) is located nearby.

CÚCUTA

Cúcuta ⓴ is the capital of Norte de Santander Department and, located a mere 16km (10 miles) from the border, and as such, is the closest major hub to Venezuela in the region. The city is notable for its tree-lined streets that provide a nice respite from heat, which tends to average around 84°F (29°C). The city was founded in 1733 and its population has since grown steadily to around 600,000 – a far cry from its dusty border town beginnings. Famous sites in town include the **Catedral de San José** (Avenida 5 Norte, no. 10–73), which sits at the east end of Parque Santander, and the **Casa de la Cultura** (Calle 13, no. 3–67; tel: 7-571 6689; Mon–Fri 8.30am–noon, 3–6pm), which houses a museum dedicated to Cúcuta's rich history, including exhibits on the War for Independence.

Santander Square in Cúcuta

ZONA CAFETERA

East of Bogotá and south of Medellín, there lies rolling green hills and high-altitude mountains that enjoy a tropical climate, making this area the premier coffee-growing region of Colombia.

Collectively, the departments of Risaralda, Caldas, and Quindío make up what is known as the axis of the Zona Cafetera—the region where Colombia's world-renowned coffee is produced.

⊙ BORDER CONSIDERATIONS

Exit and entry formalities between Colombia and Venezuela are handled at the Cúcuta office of **Migracion Colombia** (Avenida 1, no. 28–57; tel: 7-573 5210; www.migracioncolombia.gov.co; daily 8am–noon, 2–5pm). Despite Venezuela's ongoing economic difficulties, the border remains open. However, US residents need to apply for and receive a visa in their home country before entering Venezuela. To enter Colombia, foreigners must first obtain an exit stamp from Venezuelan immigration and then a Colombian entry stamp at the migration office. To enter Venezuela, foreigners must get their exit stamp at the migration office.

Coffee plantation, Manizales

MANIZALES

Despite being the capital of the Department of Caldas, **Manizales** ⓯ is a smallish city of about 500,000 residents. It was founded in 1848 by a group of settlers who were trying to flee a situation of civil unrest in the capital. Manizales itself was settled at an altitude of 2,150 meters (7,000ft), on the narrow saddle of a mountain with precious flatland to spare. Today Manizales is a city that is still in touch with its roots, celebrating its founders and heritage.

Navigating Manizales

The center is a good base for exploring the city. The area is good for walking, but the narrow streets are often congested with traffic. Also *telefericos* transport people up and down the streets of the sloping municipality. The main thoroughfare is Carrera 23 (sometimes called Avenida Santander), which runs from one end of the city to the other. The road then leads 8km (5 miles) southwest to La Nubia airport, and then all the way to Bogotá

In the center of Manizales is the **Plaza de Bolívar**, which features ceramic murals detailing Colombia's history, by famed local sculptor Guillermo Botero. At the north end of the plaza is **La Gobernación** (www.gobernaciondecaldas.gov.co/web; Mon–Fri 7am–5pm), a neocolonial government building with one of the most striking facades on the square. Perhaps the only other building on the plaza that eclipses it is the enormous **Cathedral Basílica Metropolitana de Nuestra Señora del Rosario** (Basilica Cathedral of Our Lady of the Rosary of Manizales; Carrera 22; tel: 6-883 1880), which is designed in the neo-Gothic style. If you travel along Avenida 12 de Octubre you will reach the **Parque Chipre**, which affords great views of the city to the east, and of coffee country to the west. Also here is the **Monumento a los Colonizadores**, a monument to the colonists of the area made from melted-down keys

El Cable

If you follow Carrera 23 east in the direction of Bogotá, you'll eventually reach Calle 65 and the **old cableway terminal**. This old cable line was in operation from 1922 until the 1960s, and acted as an easy means for shipping coffee over the 3,700-meter (12,140-ft) Alto de Las Letras pass. Today this area is known as **El Cable**, and it is Manizales' Zona Rosa, filled with upscale bars and trendy restaurants.

PARQUE ECOLÓGICO RÍO BLANCO

Just a few kilometers northwest of Manizales is the **Parque Ecológico Río Blanco** ⓰ (tel: 6-887 9770), a protected cloud forest covering 4,932 hectares (12,187 acres). This might be the best spot for birdwatching in a country already famous for great

Coffee in Manizales

Manizales is the epicenter of coffee production in the region, and some of the best haciendas can be found just outside of town. With coffee prices declining in recent decades, many farms have been forced to open their doors to visitors, and coffee tours have become big business. From Manizales most hotels and hostels will arrange excursions to the haciendas.

birding sites. There are more than 350 known species here, including 33 species of hummingbird, four kinds of toucan, the royal woodpecker, and a rare type of rusty-faced parrot. There are also 40 different types of orchids and 350 species of butterfly.

PEREIRA

Located 56km (35 miles) southwest of Manizales, **Pereira** ⑰ is the service capital of the coffee zone and the official capital of Risaralda Department. This city of around 475,000 people sits on a plateau at an altitude of 1,411 meters (4,629ft) and makes a nice spot to visit: it's less touristy than Manizales and the surrounding countryside is just as beautiful. From the city you can see all the way to the peaks of the Cordillera Central. Two rivers bind the city: the Río Otún in the north and the Río Consota in the south.

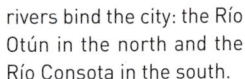

The center of the city revolves around the **Plaza de Bolívar**, and visitors can walk to most points of interest from here. The areas between Carreras 10 and 12, as well as east-facing streets like Calle 14, are known for high crime rates, and are therefore best avoided.

Hummingbird in Río Blanco Reserve

SALENTO

On the road toward Parque Los Nevados, in the foothills

of the Cordillera Central, is the little town of **Salento** ⓲. It sits at 1,985 meters (6,500ft) above sea level and is the oldest town in the Quindío Department, having been founded in 1842. Flowers and crops flourish here, which is a direct result of the regular rainfall the area receives. To the east you can see the snow-capped peaks of Los Nevados.

There was a time when Salento was a quiet, sleepy village. Those days are long gone: today, Salento is a popular weekend destination for locals and tourists alike. People love the brightly colored houses, and the surrounding hilly countryside of the Valley de Cocora makes for great treks among the towering wax palms (Colombia's national tree). There's a stunning **central plaza** in town, with a center sculpture of a saber-wielding Bolívar, as well as a standout church, **Nuestra Señora del Carmen**.

PARQUE NACIONAL LOS NEVADOS

In central Colombia there exists a small range of volcanic peaks that make up the **Parque Nacional Los Nevados** ⓳. These peaks include the snow-covered Nevado del Ruiz, Nevado del Santa Isabel, and Nevado del Tolima. This cluster of peaks makes for great high-altitude trekking. It's a nine-hour excursion from Bogotá, or four hours if you are traveling from Manizales. Interestingly, you can actually see the snow-capped peaks of Nevado del Ruiz, the highest of all the volcanos in the range at 5,321 meters (17,457ft), from Manizales.

The national park office recommends all visitors check the seismic activity warnings at the Colombian Geological Survey (www2.sgc.gov.co) before planning their trip to Los Nevados. You must be accompanied by an approved guide on any tour or excursion to the park, which can be arranged in Manizales.

Plaza San Pedro Claver, Cartagena

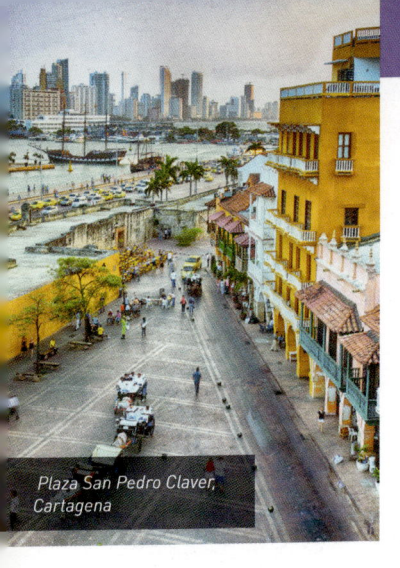

CARTAGENA

Cartagena ⓴ is located on Colombia's central Caribbean coast, where all Costeño people and traditions converge, forming one unique culture that is both homogenous and eclectic. The city is divided up into multiple sectors. Colonial Cartagena is known as El Centro (or the "walled city" or "old city"), and it sits at the north end of Bahía Cartagena, surrounded by 12km (7 miles) of old ramparts. This is where many of the most idyllic plazas, parks, and upscale boutique hotels can be found.

Budget hotels can be found in the neighborhood of Getsemaní, which has a more working-class and bohemian feel to it. Cartagena's official downtown borders Getsemaní, and the city then continues for 10km (6 miles) north, south, and east. Traveling these extended routes will lead you around the bay, and to the access points for offshore islands like Islas Rosario. If you need further assistance, be sure to stop by Cartagena's main tourist office, which is located in the **Casa del Marqués del Premio Real** on the Plaza Aduana (tel: 5-660 1583; daily 9am–6pm).

WALKING THE RAMPARTS

One of the best ways to take in Cartagena is by walking one of its most iconic features: the ramparts that encircle the old city. Typically this route takes 90 minutes, but times vary depending on where you start and how often you stop. The best place to begin is the **Baluarte San Francisco Javier A**, continuing around the Circuit to **La India Catalina B** and on past the lagoons to the Puente Román. The circuit breaks, but its final section is along the **Calle del Arsenal** and finishes at the **Playa Barahona**, which is located by the bay. Sunset and sunrise are great times to go.

GETSEMANÍ

A good anchor point for the outer city is the **Puente Román C**, which leads from Manga Island to Getsemaní. Getsemaní lies on the northwest end of the bridge and is known as the bohemian area of the city. Some notable landmarks include the **Iglesia de Santísma Trinidad D** (Church of Santísma Trinidad; Carrera 10 at Calle del Guerrero). This Holy Trinity church, located on the Plaza de la Trinidad, was completed around 1643. Along Calle 25, toward the entrance to the old city, is the **Convento San Francisco E**, a monastery founded in 1555. In 1610 it became the first seat of the Spanish inquisitors, and it's on the courtyard where a crowd declared independence from Spain on November 11, 1811. San Francisco is located just south of the arches leading into the walled city (the Puerta del Reloj).

THE WALLED CITY

Walk through the Puerta del Reloj from Getsemaní and you'll arrive at the **Plaza de los Coches F**. Originally this was the site of the slave market, but then it became a sort-of transportation hub for embarking carriages. Inside the plaza's long arcades you'll find the Portal de los Dulces, an outdoor confectionery store selling cookies, *dulce de coco* (coconut brittle), and much more.

Just south and around the corner from Los Coches is the **Plaza de la Aduana G**, which features a large white statue of Christopher Columbus. Behind the plaza are the **Palacio**

Municipal and the **Casa del Marqués del Premio Real**, which was the onetime home of the King's representative from Spain. On the corner is the **Museo de Arte Moderno** ❽ (Museum of Modern Art; tel: 5-664 5815; www.mamcartagena.org; Mon–Fri 9am–noon, Sun 4pm–9pm; free last Sun of month), a two-story museum focusing mostly on Latin American art from the 1950s onward.

A 17th-century Jesuit church and monastery, the **San Pedro Claver** ❶ (Mon–Fri 8am–5.30pm, Sun 8am–5pm) is located near the museum at **Plaza San Pedro**. It is named after a local monk, Peter Claver, who was known as El Apóstol de los Negros (The Apostle of the Blacks) as he supported the liberation of slaves. Claver died in 1654 and was canonized in 1896 by Pope Leo XVIII. His body is kept over the altar in a glass coffin. Nearby, at the corner of Calle Ricaurte, is the old **Convento Santa Teresa**, a convent founded in 1609 for Carmelite nuns. It is today the luxurious Charleston Santa Teresa Hotel.

Other sites worth visiting in the old city include **El Bodegón de la Candelaria** ❿ (Calle Las Dama, no. 3–64), a restored colonial house that's over 300 years old. The green and leafy **Plaza de Bolívar** is located one block away and features an equestrian statue of the Liberator. Impromptu shows often occur here, and if you're lucky you may see some cumbia dancers from the Palenque region just south of Cartagena moving to the coastal rhythms.

On the west side of the plaza is the **Palacio de la Inquisición** ⓚ (Mon–Fri 9am–6pm), the premises where the Inquisition operated. The current building dates from 1706 and, all told some 800 people were sentenced to death on this site for 'Crimes against the Christian Faith.' The various torture and execution implements on display inside serve as a reminder of the building's violent past.

Across the street from the plaza is the long, white **Palacio de la Proclamación** ⓛ, which is named after the proclamation of the declaration of independence and was once a governor's residence. Nearby is the **Convento Santo Domingo** M, regarded in some circles as the oldest church in Cartagena, with constructing beginning around 1551. Inside the church, behind a Baroque 19th-century altar, there is a 16th-century carving of Christ. Adjacent to the church is the **Plaza Santo Domingo**, which might be the busiest section of the old city, with many outdoor cafes and bars.

Plaza Santo Domingo

Walk along Baudillo (Carrera 7) and you'll arrive at the **Iglesia Santo Toribio de Mogrovejo** N. It has a Baroque altar and, interestingly, you can still see the damage caused by a cannonball that went through the church in 1741 and lodged in the west wall. Last but not least, book lovers will want to visit the **Casa de Gabriel García Márquez** O (located behind the Santa Clara Hotel), on the corner of Calle del Curato. This was the Cartagena home of Colombia's favorite son, and it makes sense that the born Costeño made his home in the historic heart of the Colombian coast.

BOCAGRANDE

Bocagrande is where colonial Cartagena ends and the modern metropolis takes over. The area is less than one kilometer (just over half a mile) from the walled city, yet it feels a million miles

Playa Blanca

away. Shimmering apartment buildings, hotels, and condominiums jut into the sky, and tower cranes are ever at work erecting new homes for Colombia's privileged elite. On the southern tip of the area is the Fuerte Castillo Grande, which was built to protect Cartagena's inner harbor. To get to Bocagrande take a bus heading south from the entrance to the walled city, the Puerto del Reloj.

ISLA TIERRABOMBA AND ISLA DE BARÚ

In the south, between Bocagrande and Isla de Barú is **Isla Tierrabomba**, an island that acts as a natural barrier between Cartagena and the open sea. **Fuerte San Fernando** overlooks the bay from the southern tip of the island, and nearby **Isla de Barú** has the **Fuerte San José**. At one time these two forts were connected by chains in order to dissuade pirate attacks. Isla de Barú is the closest island to Cartagena, and one that is linked via road as well as by waterways. The tourist boats stop at **Playa Blanca**, the most famous beach in the area. Its pristine white sands and crystalline waters are the reasons people come here. Various companies at the tourist dock in Cartagena sell transportation tickets that vary in price. However, you should be paying around US$20 for tickets to Islas del Rosario and Playa Blanca. Be aware that there is also a port tax of US$6.

CARIBBEAN COAST

The roots of Colombia as a nation can be traced directly to its Caribbean coastline. It was on this area of South America's coastline that the first Spanish explorers arrived, and it is at modern day Santa Marta where the first official settlement was founded. It was from these shores that Spanish armies first moved down the Magdalena River toward the Andes, in search of gold and the famed lost city of El Dorado. It was also here that the Spanish built a great fortress city to protect their spoils, Cartagena de Indias. When revolutionary fever swept the country, some of the most critical battles, power grabs, and gambits played out in the theater of the Caribbean.

BARRANQUILLA

Barranquilla ㉑ is a thriving port city of about a million residents that is ever growing and ever expanding. If you are arriving by land then you will likely find yourself at the **Terminal de Transportes Metropolitano** (Carrera 14, no. 54–98; tel: 5-323 0034; www.ttbaq.com.co), the bus terminal located in the far south of town. To travel locally by bus, you can take the Transmetro, which runs north through the center and into the north of the city along the river.

Barranquilla Carnival

Barranquilla is where Colombia holds its own version of Carnival (www.carnavaldebarranquilla.org) – second only in size and scope to the one in Brazil. 40 days before Easter, at the end of February or the beginning of March, this city becomes the scene of the country's biggest party.

Central Barranquilla

In the center you'll find the historic heart of Barranquilla, the **Plaza**

San Nicolas. The standout here is the neo-Gothic **Catedral San Nicolás de Tolentino** (Carrera 42, no. 33–45), which sits at the west end of the plaza. A few blocks north of the Plaza is the **Paseo Bolívar** B [map], a wide pedestrian-only throughway along Calle 34. At the end of the Paseo, at Carrera 46, is the **Museo del Caribe** (Calle 36, no. 46–66; tel: 5-372 0581; www.culturacaribe.org; Tue–Thu 8am–5pm, Fri 8am–6pm, Sat–Sun 9am–6pm). This blocky grey monolith features indigenous artifacts, with exhibits dating from Spanish colonization to more recent times.

Further northwest you'll find one of the true gems of the city, the **Museo Romantico** (Carrera 54, no. 59–199; daily 8am–5pm). The museum is housed in a lovely old Republican mansion that was donated by a wealthy family, and features various items detailing the history of Barranquilla, including a number of Carnival costumes. There's also a room dedicated to Colombian literary hero Gabriel García Márquez that features some of his notes, first editions, and typewriters.

SANTA MARTA

Modern Santa Marta is the site of the official first Spanish settlement in Colombia, having been founded by the conquistador Rodrigo de Bastidas back in 1525. Today, **Santa Marta** ㉒ is the capital of Magdalena Department, and most of this bay city is comprised of working-class residential neighborhoods and budget shopping districts. However, it is also a thriving tourist destination due to its central beach and idyllic neighbor, the charming fishing village of Taganga.

Walking the central promenade you'll notice that Santa Marta hasn't forgotten its indigenous residents. There are various statues by the water celebrating Tairona heritage, including one on the south end of town, at Carrera 1 and Calle 22, called **La Herencia Tairona**, which features a proud indigenous couple holding court over their place in the world. The best place to get your bearings around here is at Carrera 1 and Calle 15. This is the center of Santa Marta, and if you head east on Calle 15 you'll pass right along Plaza Bolívar.

The center

This is where you'll find all the grand plazas, old colonial buildings, and museums for which the city is famous. The expansive

Barranquilla Carnival

and leafy **Plaza Bolívar**, complete with an equestrian statue of the Liberator, is a good base for exploring other parts of the city. Nearby to the plaza is one of the oldest buildings in Santa Marta, the **Casa de la Aduana**, which is now the **Museo del Oro** (Calle 14, no. 2-07; tel: 5-421 0251; Tue–Sat 9am–5pm, Sun 10am–3pm; free). This old colonial customs house dates back to 1531, but the museum it now houses was inaugurated in 2014. The museum showcases the history of Santa Marta through multiple exhibits over two floors. It features many pre-Columbian archeological finds, such as ceramics and gold work produced by the indigenous Tairona people.

Out of all the colonial churches in Colombia, the bright white **Catedral Basilíca de Santa Marta** (Carrera 4, no. 16-02; mass times: Mon–Fri noon and 6pm, Sun 7am, 10am, noon and 6pm) might be the most impressive. It sits on the former site of what is said to be the first Catholic church in Colombia. However, the church that stands here today was finished in 1766. The church held the remains of The Liberator, Simón Bolívar, from his death in 1830 until they were transferred to Venezuela in 1842.

The Quinta de San Pedro Alejandrino

The **Quinta de San Pedro** (Avenida Del Libertador s/n; tel: 301-241 5913; daily 9am–4:30pm; open later during high season), a small villa on a former 17th-century sugar plantation, is where the great Liberator, Simón Bolívar, spent his final days. The museum is little more than the home with the room where Bolívar spent his final hours as he was dying of tuberculosis, and includes a few personal items. Paintings and memorabilia from the 18th and 19th centuries are also on display here.

RODADERO

Despite the tourist bars, nightclubs and restaurants, Santa Marta is more of a laidback colonial city. The more modern and vibrant **Rodadero** ㉓, located just 4km (2 miles) south of Santa Marta (minibuses run between Santa Marta and Rodadero, leaving from Carrera 1), is where you can find the hustle and bustle. The seemingly endless **Rodadero Beach** is lined with high-rise hotels and restaurants (all serving solid *pescados* and *mariscos*). Much of the beach is tree-lined, providing welcome shade, and street vendors roam the promenade selling drinks and seafood cocktails. At night you'll find people lining the *embarcadero*, blasting music, drinking, and co-mingling. It's a great time, but you should also look out for petty crime.

TAGANGA

Located 3km (2 miles) north of Santa Marta is the picturesque fishing village of **Taganga** ㉔ (15 minutes by bus, leaving from Carrera 1 in Santa Marta). The pace of life is still slow here,

Rodadero Beach

but recently development and the tourism boom have knocked most of the sleepiness out of the village, as its streets are now prowling with backpackers and vacationers. Just north and around the corner from Taganga is **Playa Grande**, another quasi-secluded beach perfect for a day of lazing, drinking and eating. Continue east along the coast from Taganga and you'll reach the stunning **Parque Nacional Tayrona.**

PARQUE NACIONAL TAYRONA

One of the most beautiful protected areas in the country, **Parque Nacional Natural Tayrona** ㉕ (park hours 8am–5pm) runs 85km (53 miles) north along the coast from Tagonga, just outside of Santa Marta. Most of this stretch is still undeveloped, and just offshore are any number of coral reefs. Snorkeling is good here, and the best spots are Cabo San Juan de Guia and the smaller La Piscina beach.

This has long been a region of great spiritual significance to the coastal Colombian indigenous cultures of today and generations past. The indigenous Kogi tribe (descendants of the Tairona people) still have authority over Parque Nacional Tayrona. Consequently, they typically close it once a year (usually February) for one month for spiritual cleansing purposes.

Getting there

Buses leave every 15 minutes or so from the **Mercado Publico** (Calle 2, no.8–81), and head to the El Zaino entrance of Parque Nacional Tayrona. However, most people visiting the park choose to book a package through local providers, and head out in private transport: once you arrive at the El Zaino entrance, it's still a long way to the nearest beach. If you choose to take another bus from the entrance, they'll drop you off near to Cañaveral Beach.

CIUDAD PERDIDA AND EL PUEBLITO

Out of all of the indigenous archeological sites in Colombia, none are as famous as **Ciudad Perdida** ㉖ (the Lost City). This 13-hectare (32-acre) city was located deep in the Sierra Nevada Mountains, and at its height was home to up to 2,400 Tairona indigenous people, who lived in round houses set on stone-paved terraces. An even larger – although slightly less awe-inspiring – former city and archeological site, known as **El Pueblito** ㉗, is located nearer to the coast and was probably home to around 3,000 Tairona people. Today you can visit both of these archeological sites by booking treks from tour operators in Santa Marta.

Cabo San Juan del Guia, Tayrona National Park

GUAJIRA

You'll know you've arrived in Guajira when the green of the Sierra Nevada de Santa Marta Mountains gives way to desolate expanses of land home to little other plant life than cacti and the stout *trupillo* tree. Guajira extends to the self-named peninsula, which marks the northernmost tip of South America. As with Tierra del Fuego in southernmost Argentina, arriving here feels not just like you've encountered the end of a continent, but the end of the world. Guajira is home to the Wayúu people, Colombia's largest indigenous group.

RIOHACHA

Travel 160km (100 miles) east along the coast from the colonial town of Santa Marta and you'll arrive in what feels like fishing village, yet just happens to be a department capital. **Riohacha** ㉖. It may not look much on the surface but on weekends, when its people come out to play, it becomes a lively city. Most important is that Riohacha is a gateway to the Wayúu culture.

The city is mostly known for its long wooden pier that divides the town's two principal white-sand beaches. While you're in Riohacha you should make time to visit the town's old **municipal market** (Mon 6am–6pm, Sun 6am–noon), located in the center, and the more **modern market**, located in south Riohacha. Most people who come to Riohacha will likely be passing through on their way to the northern Guajira coast, or even on into Venezuela.

Traveling to and from Riohacha

Transportation is shoddy and sporadic in Guajira. There are more buses to/from Riohacha in the morning than the afternoon, although there are private transportation options for excursions to Cabo de la Vela and farther north. Be warned that any excursion to the remote parts of Guajira can be a time-consuming proposition. Taxis can take you as far north as the outposts of Uribía and Manaure, and from there its dirt roads all the way to Cabo de la Vela and beyond. It's best to book a tour to these areas from Riohacha, and they typically last three days.

PALOMINO

Palomino ㉙ may be small, but it is exploding in popularity as much as any other coastal hotbed in Colombia. New hotels and hostels are being built all the time in order to keep up with the influx of visitors. It's not difficult to see why people flock here: it's tranquil, there's a river running right into the ocean, and it affords great views of the Sierra Nevada Mountains, including Pico Bolívar.

Mostly people come for the beach. It has become very popular in recent years with visitors on the hunt for Colombia's lesser-known Caribbean coast beaches. This one is long and inviting, and not nearly as crowded as anything you'll find near Cartagena and Santa Marta (for now). There are strong currents here, though, so watch out for red flags on the beach denoting riptides.

SANTUARIO LOS FLAMENCOS

Some 25km (15 miles) west of Riohacha, the national park of **Santuario de Fauna y Flora Los Flamencos** ㉚ covers 7,000 hectares (17,300 acres) of mostly mangrove swamps. The saline vegetation here is an attractive spot for flamingos, and whole colonies of these birds have made it their home. The area is dotted with indigenous Wayúu communities and the park guides all come from these villages. The Wayúu rely on the plantlife in the area for a number of purposes, including everything from soap and shampoo substitutes to cholesterol-lowering wonder cacti. It's possible to arrange nature tours through local hostels in Riohacha, for around US$5 and lasting roughly one hour.

URIBÍA

Riohacha may be the official capital of the department, but **Uribía** ⓛ, located where the mangroves and lakes east of Santa Marta finally give way to the parched desert of the northern peninsula, is the indigenous capital of the country. The 14,000 residents of the town are mostly all of Wayúu descent, as are the nearly 100,000 that live in the areas surrounding Uribía. Upon arriving in Uribía, you'll notice a marked change in the weather: the wind here is furious. Many older residents of northern Guajira wear the effects of the elements, with weather-beaten and sun-scorched faces.

Palomino beach at sunrise

For most travelers, Uribía serves merely as a transition point between Riohacha and the northern coastal areas including Cabo de la Vela and Punta Gallinas. Transportation to these destinations leaves Uribía from the central **Plaza Bolívar**, across from the cemetery. Seats in a four-wheel-drive jeep from Uribía to Cabo de la Vela can be purchased for around US$7 (one way). If you are making this journey, it is best to set off for the coast in the morning. However there are transportation options all day.

> ### The Wayúu Festival
>
> One reason outsiders should come to Uribía specifically is to enjoy the biggest indigenous festival in the country: The Wayúu Festival. This occurs in May and locals celebrate their heritage with dance, song, and plenty of authentic food. The people couldn't be friendlier, but ask their permission before taking a photograph. For more information, see www.colombia.travel/en/fairs-and-festivals/wayuu-cultural-festival.

CABO DE LA VELA

In **Cabo de la Vela** ③, on the northern Guajira coast, turquoise waters lap at a scorched desert shore, making the cape at once beckoning and forbidding. Even the harsh breezes can't drive away the fun; in fact, they facilitate it. Offshore winds form the perfect conditions for kite-surfing, and it's the premier activity in this little town of 1,800.

The town is small enough that you can traverse it end-to-end, seeing everything there is to see in about 30 minutes or so. In the center are mostly *hospedajes* that double as restaurants. At the most easterly end of the cape, past Refugio Sau Ipa, is a lookout point topped by a wooden cross. It's a great and quick hike to the top, where you can survey all of Cabo de la Vela to the west.

PUNTA GALLINAS

Many people make the trek from Uribía to **Punta Gallinas** ③ to spend time at this unique spot, which is the northernmost point on the South American continent. There is little here except scattered indigenous communities and some of the most striking landscapes on the planet. There are few places in South America where you'll feel closer to the end of the world; but when you leave the beach and dive into the perfectly warm ocean, you'll never feel closer to it. Tours here can be booked to and from Punta Gallinas from either Uribía or Cabo de la Vela.

PARQUE NACIONAL NATURAL MACUIRA

At the **Parque Nacional Natural Macuira** ㉞, you'll find tropical jungle and desert – in almost exactly the same place. This 250 sq km (96 sq mile) area is known locally as the Serranía de Macuira (named after the Wayúu's ancestors, the Makui) and it exists because of unique geography. The area sits at around 550 meters (1,800ft) above sea level. High levels of humidity here form the conditions necessary to produce lush vegetation and elfin cloud forest. Moisture comes in from the northeast, creating clouds at night that dissipate in the morning, resulting in about 450mm (18ins) of annual precipitation that feeds the rivers running through the park, all of which all evaporate once they reach the desert sand.

You can only enter the park with a local indigenous guide. Guides can be found in the park's surrounding settlements, such as Nazareth. There's a park-information cabin

Unspoiled beach near Punta Gallinas

Wayùu people living on the Guajira Peninsula

in Nazareth, which also has a camping space. Some Wayúu in the surrounding settlements will let you hang a hammock on their property, and some of the settlements offer basic food. However, it's best to stock up on provisions in the last real town, which is Uribía.

MAICAO

The Caribbean Coastal Highway 90 continues from Riohacha east for 90 minutes to the border city of **Maicao** ㉟. This hub is mostly a transition and stopping point for those traveling to and from the Venezuelan border. The town's commerce is made up of mostly clothing and textiles, and after dark most of the activity ceases and the streets become unsafe. There is a large Middle Eastern population here, resulting from mass immigration in the 1930s. In 1997 they founded one of the largest mosques in Latin America: the Mosque of Omar Ibn Al-Khattab.

The Venezuelan border is located 8km (5 miles) east of Maicao at the town of **Paraguachón**. It's best to take care of all visa requirements at the Venezuelan consulate in Cartagena Bocagrande, (Carrera 3, Edificio Centro Ejecutivo, Piso 14 Of. 14-02; tel: 7-665 0353; Mon–Fri 9am–noon, 1.30–4pm) or in Barranquilla (Carrera 52, no. 69–96. Edificio Concasa. piso 03; tel: 5-368 2207; www.barranquilla.consulado.gob.ve;

Mon–Thu 8am–noon, 1.30pm–4pm, Fri 8am–noon). There is no Venezuelan consul in Maicao and there have been reports of unreliability at the office in Riohacha. If you are interested in a transit visa you will need to show proof of an onward ticket to a third country within three days. If you are a US citizen you must apply for a visa at a Venezuelan embassy in the United States before attempting to cross the border. At the border, Venezuelan immigration is open daily 6am–9pm, and Colombian immigration is open daily from 8am–5pm.

For other immigration formalities contact Migración Colombia in Riohacha (Calle 5, no. 4-48; www.migracioncolombia.gov.co; Mon–Fri 8am–noon, 2–5pm).

SAN ANDRÉS ISLAND

Some 770km (480 miles) north of Colombia is a remote archipelago, dubbed the 'Sea of Seven Colors' by locals. The 11km (7-mile)-long island of **San Andrés** 36 may be small, but it has a rich history. In the 17th century, English ship owners brought West African slaves to the island via Jamaica to work the cotton and tobacco fields. Soon the Spanish attacked and the pirates followed

Practicalities

The island's long distance from Colombia means the only practical way to get there is to fly. Be aware that upon arrival at the Gustavo Rojas Pinilla International Airport all foreigners are required to purchase a tourist card for around US$33. Do not lose it, as you will need to present it on your return flight. The card is also required if you wish to travel to neighboring Isla Providencia. Inter-island travel from San Andrés to Providencia Island is relatively easy, with cargo ships leaving the main *muelle* (dock) at the north end of the island.

hot on their heels. San Andrés appealed to pirates because it made for a strategic base of operations from which to launch raids on mainland cities and settlements – as well as attacks on Spanish galleons, which were loaded with gold.

All of this history has led San Andrés to become what it is today: a Unesco-declared Biosphere Reserve that boasts some of the most stunning beaches anywhere in the Caribbean, as well as world-class diving off the third-largest barrier reef in the world. It's also a cultural hotbed, with about 50 percent of the 80,000-strong population representing immigrants from the mainland, while the remaining 50 percent are comprised of descendants of Jamaican slaves whose genealogy is a mix of early French, Dutch, Spanish, and English settlers. In fact, the original Creole English is still spoken on the island today.

Johnny Cay

This is the most iconic atoll in San Andrés —the one that you literally see on all the postcards. Fast water taxis leave from

⊙ DIVING SAN ANDRÉS AND PROVIDENCIA

On San Andrés Island you'll find good diving conditions, with depths ranging from three to 30 meters (10–100ft), and visibility from 30–60 meters (100–200ft). Some good sites here include Black Coral Net and Morgan's Sponge. For deep water diving, try the Pared Azul (Blue Wall). For Providencia, some good dive sites at Old McBean Lagoon include Manta's Place (filled with the titular mantas), Felipe's Place (where you'll find a well-preserved underwater statue of Christ), and Stairway to Heaven, famous for its large coral wall the **Muelle Casa de la Cultura** (Pier; Carrera 1, no. 21) and stop at the best cays: first to El Acuario and Haynes Cay, and then to Johnny Cay. The boats leave daily at 9am and 11am, returning at 3.30pm, costing around US$10 for the round trip. Upon disembarking at Johnny Cay, you must pay an entrance tax of around US$3 to help maintain the island.

Johnny Cay.

The east side of San Andrés

Those who want to get away from the relative hustle and bustle of San Andrés' commercial district should head to the east side of the island. There are a number of cays located just offshore, as well as the rusted out hulks of once-great tankers. There are some small, quieter towns here and the beaches, like **Playa Rocky Cay,** are just as stunning as anything you'll find on the north side of the island. There are also plenty of waterfront resorts for those who want to bask in the sun and enjoy the good life.

PROVIDENCIA

Providencia ㊲ is a small island just 7km (4 miles) long and 3.5km (2 miles) wide, with only about 5,000 residents. It's a volcanic island instead of coral, meaning it's greener than San Andres (and also features scene stealers like waterfalls). Also, where San Andrés is more developed, Providencia has blocked most mainland and foreign operators from building. That means you'll find fewer lodging options as well. The few hotels that do exist here can be found on the west side at **Bahia Augadulce**.

At the southwest end of the island you'll find its two most famous beaches: **Bahia Manzanillo** and **Bahia Sur Oeste**. They are long, palm-lined beaches abundant in white sand and little else. To the north, you'll find the famous **Isla Santa Catalina**, a former pirate hideout separated from the mainland by a narrow channel. There are boat trips around the island, but you can also walk to it via a 100-meter bridge called the Punete de Los Amantes (Lover's Bridge).

Old Providence McBean Lagoon
On the east of the island is where you'll also find Colombia's only national park on this archipelago, the **Parque Nacional Old Providence McBean Lagoon** (www.parquesnacionales.gov.co), which was created here in 1966. The park was specifically setup to protect the reef of the same name, which at 32km (20 miles) long, is the third-largest barrier reef in the world. At **Cabo Congrejo** (Crab Cay), you will be required to pay an entrance fee of around US$5. This idyllic little outcropping is a great place for snorkeling and swimming. Toward the southern end of the national park you'll find **Cayos Tres Hermanos**, notable for its surrounding light blue and crystalline waters.

CALI

Cali ❸ is located south of Antioquia, in the Valle de Cauca, west of the Cauca River. More than anything, the city of some three million is famous for dancing. It has anointed itself the "Salsa capital of Colombia," and it's difficult to argue against it. Cali is home to the largest salsa festival in the country (and indeed the world) – the Festival Mundial de Salsa. While the best salsa bars can be found around Barrio Menga or Barrio Juanchito in the northeastern part of town, there are some great individual spots all over the city (just ask any local). The main night to go out dancing is Thursday. For more local info on where to go, visit www.comoespahoy.com.co.

Salsa academy in Cali

The city center

Parque Simón Bolívar should be the anchor point for visitors to Cali. It is near to the colonial heart of the city and hugs the Cauca River. You can find your way anywhere around town using this park as your baseline. A couple of blocks to the south of Parque Bolívar you'll find one of the most impressive colonial sites in the city, the **Iglesia de San Francisco** (Church and Monastery of San Francisco). The church dates to the mid-18th century and has a stunning ornate ceiling surrounded by many carvings, images, and paintings.

A couple blocks west you'll find two art galleries housed in a former convent: the **Museo de Arte Colonial** (actually part of the church; Mon-Fri 9am–12pm 2–5pm, Sat 9am–12pm), which features a collection of 16th and 17th century paintings, and the **Museo Arqueológico** (Archeological Museum; Carrera 4, no. 6–59; tel: 2-885 4675; Mon–Sat 9am–1pm, 2–6pm). Here you'll find interesting

La Ermita

collections of pre-Columbian pottery from the Calima indigenous group.

Over by the river, at the intersection of Carrera 1 and Calle 13, is one of the standout churches in the city, **La Ermita** (mass: Mon–Sat 7.30am and 5pm, Sun 10am and 5pm), a neo-Gothic cathedral painted blue and bright white. The original church that sat on this site was built in 1602 and influenced by the cathedral in Cologne, Germany.

SAN ANTONIO AND THE WEST

South of the river and to the west lies the neighborhood of **San Antonio**, which is regarded as the bohemian heart of Cali. Like La Candelaria in Bogotá, San Antonio is located in the hills. One of the most popular treks is to make your way up Carreras 5 and 10, through neighborhoods of lovely Colonial homes up to the **Capilla San Antonio** (San Antonio Chapel; 2-658 0022), a humble 18th-century church that appears little changed since it was founded in 1747. Most people come here for the sunset views of Cali as seen from the park in front of the plaza.

North of San Antonio you'll find the **Museo de Arte Moderno La Tertulia** (Museum of Modern Art La Tertulia; Carrera 1, no, 5–105; tel: 2-893-2939; www.museolatertulia.com; Tue–Sun 10am–8pm, Sun 2–6pm), which has some

1,500 pieces of South American art spread over three floors. To the west of this museum is the zoo, the **Zoológico de Cali** (tel: 2-488 0888; www.zoologicodecali.com.co; daily 9am–4pm), which creatively incorporates the river in its exhibits. From here, head west for one of the best *miradors* (lookouts) in the city, the **Monumento Cristo Rey**. Sitting on a 1,470-meter (4,800ft) -high hill, this Christ Statue affords stunning panoramic views over Cali.

THE NORTH AND EAST

Another great *mirador* in Cali is located in the northwest of the city. The **Monumento Las Tres Cruces** (Monument of the Three Crosses) is named for the three crosses sitting atop a 1,450-meter (4,757ft) hill. During Holy Week it's a traditional pilgrimage site that offers more great views of the city and Valle de Cauca. To the east is the **Orchideorama** (Avenida 2 Norte, no. 48-10; 665 8358; www.caliorquideas.com; Mon–Fri 8am–noon, 2–5pm), an orchid garden. The park cultivates various types of this coveted flower, and its idyllic green grounds make it a popular spot for weddings.

SOUTH OF CALI

POPAYÁN

Popayán ㊴, a city of roughly 250,000 people located around two hours' drive from Cali, still exudes the spirit of the Spanish colonial settlement that defined its earliest origins way back in 1537. As capital of the Department of Cauca, Popayán seems almost stuck in time, with its cobbled-stone streets, white-washed houses, and expansive plazas. And all of it is protected from any encroaching development by the impenetrable green mountains of the Cordillera Central that surround it.

It makes for a relaxing day trip from Cali and a good spot to relax after all that partying in the city's *salsotecas*. It's an ideal base for excursions to the archeological site of Tierradentro. Popayán is also home to a modern university scene and has a large student population. The **Catedral Basilica Nuestra Señora de la Asuncíon** (Cathedral Basilica of our Lady of the Assumption; Calle 5 at Carrera 6; daily 8.30am–6pm) is one of the most iconic buildings in the city and is as virginal white as many of the houses in the historic district. It sits on the south side of the **Plaza Mayor** (Parque Cladas) and has a long and storied history. It was inaugurated in 1537 but the latest iteration was completed in 1900 and restored again after a 1983 earthquake. The church is in neoclassical style and there's a marble Madonna behind the altar. The building itself is topped by a stately 40-meter (130ft) -high dome.

Another impressive house of worship is **La Ermita de Jesús Nazareno** (Calle 5 at Carrera 2; mass times: Mon–Sat 5pm, Sun 9:30pm and 5pm). This is the oldest church in the city, dating back to the founding of Popayán. If you're up for a walk you can head east along Calle 5 from the Plaza Mayor, past La Ermita, to the **Iglesia de Belén** (mass times: Mon–Sat 4pm, Sun 11.30am–4pm), a pleasant chapel on a hill overlooking Popayán with great views of the city.

Culture vultures should head to the **Museo de Historia Natural** (Museum of Natural History; Calle 2, no. 1a–25; tel: 8-209 800; Mon–Sun 9am–11am, 2–4pm), which has eight rooms featuring educational displays on the natural history of the area, including geology and archeology. Other museums include the **Casa Museo Negret** (Calle 5a, no. 10–23; tel: 2-824 4546; Mon–Fri 8am–12pm, 2–6pm), which celebrates a single subject, one of the city's most famous residents, the artist Edgar Negret. The museum contains some of his artwork, sculptures, and photographs, plus some other works by Latin American artists.

TIERRADENTRO

Tierradentro ❿ is one of the most interesting pre-Columbian archeological sites in Colombia due to its ancient manmade *hypogea* (burial caves) that were created between the 6th and 10th centuries. They were built as tombs, not for ordinary members of Tierradentro society, but for the elite. The burial areas, which range in size from small and shallow to about 8 meters (26ft) deep, feature spiral staircases and walls decorated by the builders with black, white, and red

Popayán

geometric patterns. The various ancient sites, as well as the stunning views of the surrounding Cordillera Central, are why Tierradentro is a Unesco World Heritage Site.

Tierradentro is located in Inza, Cauca Department, which is a 100km (62-mile) -trip northeast of Popayán. It's something of a rough road but the spectacular mountain scenery makes it all worthwhile. You can leave for the sites from Inza village on horseback, although a guide is required. Hiring a guide and horse for the day will cost roughly US$15–20. You can also walk but be sure to take plenty of water, sunscreen, and a hat. There are five principal burial sites of note: Segovia, El Tablon, El Duende, Alto de San Andrés, and El Aguacate.

PASTO AND THE FAR SOUTH

The capital of the Department of Nariño, some 388km (240 miles) south of Cali, is Pasto, which was founded in 1539 by Lorenzo de Aldana. It's a robust city of some 500,000 inhabitants sitting at 2,527 meters (8,290ft) above sea level on a high plateau. Many visitors pass through here on their way to Ecuador, as the border is only 88km (55 miles) away.

The main plaza in **Pasto** is the **Parque Antonio Nariño**. Here you'll find the **Iglesia de San Juan Batista** (Mon–Fri 7.30am–11am, Sat 3.30–6.30pm, Sun 7.30am–1am), which, founded in 1537 is the oldest church in Pasto. Also in the city center is the **Museo Alfonso Zambrano** (Calle 20, no. 29–79; tel: 2-731 2837; Mon–Sat 8am–noon, 2–4pm; free), which has a nice collection of colonial and indigenous art with a focus on Quiteño (those from Quito) pieces.

IPIALES

Those heading south to Ecuador will stop in at **Ipiales** ㊶, the last major town before the border. It's about a 2-hour trip, and nearby is one of the most striking churches anywhere, **Santuario Las Lejas** (7km/4 miles from Ipiales; www.santuariolavirgendelaslajas.com). Its origins are mystical as supposedly it's built on the site of a cave with healing properties. The church was first built in 1899 but it wasn't finished until 50 years later. It's located on the side of a gorge and is one of the greatest examples of Gothic Revival architecture in Colombia, maybe even the world.

Ipiales is 2km (1 mile) from the Rumichaca Bridge, which crosses the Río Carchi, and forms the border with Ecuador. Buses and *colectivos* run from Calle 14/Carrera 11 in Ipiales to the border, for around US$1. A taxi should cost between US$5–7. For visa issues contact the **Ecuadorian Consulate** in Ipiales, located in the **Oficina Migracion** (Carrera 7, no. 14–10; tel: 1-773 2292; Mon–Fri 9am–noon, 2–5pm).

CHOCÓ

On the Pacific coast of Colombia, the Chocó Department stretches 400km (250 miles) west from the Cordillera Occidental to the port city of Buenaventura and the Pacific Coast. The coastline continues north over 1,400km (870 miles) up to Panama. In this northern region you'll find the only break in the 48,000km

Santuario Las Lejas

Humpback whale, Nuquí

(29,825-mile)-long Pan-American Highway: Panama's Darién Province. Where this area meets Colombia is where the Chocó begins.

For a long time, Chocó was known more for crime than tourism. In the 1990s and 2000s, when the rebel groups were forced out of the cities by Colombia's military, they fled to remote areas like the Chocó. It appealed to rebel groups who wanted to continue their cocaine production in little-developed areas, under cover of rainforest, and with a negligible military presence. In settling here, the rebels seized land from local *campesinos*, poverty-stricken families, and other residents, forcing mass migrations of displaced Colombians (many of whom are Afro-Colombians) that continue to plague the country.

However, tourism is indeed on the upswing. Colombia's ongoing peace process means that the country might be able to stem the refugee problem in the near future. Also, the nature here is objectively stunning. In the northern Chocó are the Serranía de los Saltos and Serranía del Baudó mountain ranges, which seem to rise straight out of the Pacific Ocean and reach heights of some 500 meters (1,640ft). Whale watching is a popular tourist activity, too. You'll want to be in the coastal village of **Nuquí** during the June to October, when it's not uncommon to see pods of humpback whales breach the jade waters off Colombia's Pacific Coast.

Transportation within Chocó

As it stands, the only road services in the Chocó exist from Medellín to Quibdó. The bus company Rapido Ochoa (tel: 574-444-8888; www.rapidoochoa.com) runs a service from Medellín to Quibdó for around US$25 and the journey takes about 7 hours. However, portions of the road leading into Chocó are unpaved, which makes for an arduous and uncomfortable journey. Instead, it is recommended to fly from Medellín to Quibdó. Satena (tel: 571-605 2222; www.satena.com) and Aerolineas Antioquia (www.ada-aero.com) offer direct flights to Quibdó as well as flights to Nuquí and Bahía Solano.

QUIBDÓ

Many travelers forgo the department capital of **Quibdó** in favor of the coastal villages. While Quibdó certainly doesn't have the cache of a Medellín or Bogotá, Its location on the banks of the Río Atrato is pleasant, and the **Catedral San Francisco de**

> ### ⊙ SAFETY CONSIDERATIONS
>
> Despite Chocó's status as being a region that is ever opening up to tourism, it's always wise to exercise caution. Check with local authorities before venturing to the capital of Quibdó to check on the current situation. Other good resources include the UK's Colombia travel advice section of the foreign travel information page (www.gov.uk), and www.visitchoco.com, which is run by the Chocó Community Tourism Alliance.

Asis (Carrera 2, no. 24a–32), which overlooks the water, is as striking as any other colonial church in the country. This church acts as both a religious and cultural touchstone for the city – it's the kick off point for the famous Fiesta de San Pacho.

The Festival of Saint Francis of Assisi (Fiesta de San Pacho)

Every year, the residents of Quibdó have a huge celebration, starting September 3. The Catedral San Francisco kicks off the month-long festivities with a Catholic opening mass. After mass the church band kicks things into a higher gear with a performance of traditional *chirimía* music. It's a rollicking, get-up-and-move folk genre that features instruments from around the globe. Eventually the party leaves the church, and the musicians take to the street, and San Pacho becomes one giant party unrivalled anywhere, save for the great carnivals of the world.

NUQUÍ

Many travelers who come to Chocó will likely be heading to **Nuquí** ㊸, before possibly continuing to Bahía Solano. That's because, aside from the **Parque Nacional Natural Utría** ㊹, Nuquí is one of the best places to spot humpback whales on the entire Pacific Coast. As a town, though, it will likely leave many visitors feeling

Parque Nacional Natural Utría

underwhelmed, with just an airstrip where the flights arrive and a couple of stores. Most people will simply be passing through, headed for the famous Pacific Coast eco-lodges to the north and south of the town.

PARQUE NACIONAL NATURAL UTRÍA

Between Bahía Solano and Nuquí you'll find the **Parque Nacional Natural Utría** (boat from El Valle or Nuquí costs around US$25 return, reserve transportation at your hotel or eco-lodge). The park encompasses a portion of Chocó rich in biodiversity and comprises some 54,000 hectares (133,437 acres), preserving several aquatic and land species of animal. On the north end of the park is the *ensenada* (inlet) that is home to most of the tourist activity. There's an abundance of marine life that likes to congregate here, including two different types of whales as well as migratory turtles and many species of bird.

About halfway up the inlet you'll find the national park headquarters. There's a visitor center here with friendly staff, maps, some exhibits of whale bones, and a restaurant. Here, you can inquire about volunteer projects. Paddling around in a kayak or canoe is the best way to explore this area, as motorboats aren't allowed past the headquarters. You can find more information about the park, as well as inquire about safety concerns, at www.parquesnacionales.gov.co, or by emailing ecoturismo@parques-nacionales.gov.co.

EL VALLE

50km (30 miles) north of Nuquí, and past the Parque Natural Utría, is **El Valle** ㊺. Located on the coast, it's a rapidly developing hotbed of tourism, not least of all because it's got what's probably the best surfing in the entire Chocó. The conditions here are also great for bodysurfing or merely swimming, and

Beach at Bahía Solano

the best part is that many of these beaches are of secluded. One beach that is generally regarded as the best is **El Amejal**, which is located to the north of town. Visitors can find sleeping options here in the form of *cabanas*. **El Tigre** is another isolated beach that's about a three-hour walk from town, or you can arrive by boat.

BAHÍA SOLANO

There's a road that cuts inland from El Valle, heading north 18km (11 miles) until you reach the coastal retreat of **Bahía Solano** ㊻. As remote as it is, this bayside town of around 10,000 people is one of the tourism centers of the Chocó. Vacationers from Medellín frequently make the trip here during the whale season, as you can see these majestic animals breaching the water from the shore. It's also not uncommon to see volunteers releasing baby turtles onto the beach near the water. Regarding activities, trekking, diving, snorkeling, whale watching, surfing, birdwatching and waterfall hikes are all popular excursions here.

LOS LLANOS AND THE AMAZONAS

Stretching across central Colombia are Los Llanos ('The Plains'), all the way from the Andes in the east, to the Amazonas in the southwest. Los Llanos are part of the wider

LOS LLANOS AND THE AMAZONAS

Orinoco river basin, and as such are sometimes referred to as the Orinoco Region (Región de la Orinoquía). Much of Los Llanos are inaccessible to visitors, but that is changing slowly. **Villavicencio**, Los Llanos' transport hub and the capital of the Meta Department, is 100km (69 miles) from Bogotà.

South of Villavicencio is Llanos' most popular attraction, and one of Colombia's most impressive ecological wonders: **Caño Cristales** ㊾, also known as 'The River of Five Colours' and 'The Rainbow River'. Caño Cristales flows through a mountain range called Serranía de la Macarena, where the Andean, Orinoco and Amazon regions all met; the river itself is home to a unique species of algae (*macarenia clavigera*), which turns it into a vibrant pink-red mass of water during the rainy season, from July to November. The area had been closed off since 1989 because of guerrilla and paramilitary action, but in 2009 tour companies began running trips here from Villavicencio and Bogotà. Try **Aventure Colombia** (http://aventurecolombia.com/en) for more details.

At Colombia's southernmost tip, where the country meets Peru and Brazil, the world's largest river cuts through a jungle ecosystem that is home to a third of the world's wildlife. **Leticia** ㊽, Colombia's southernmost town, is located here, on the Amazon River, at the borders of Colombia, Brazil,

Vaccinations for the Amazonas

Although malaria is rare in Colombia, check with your doctor before arriving to see if a course of anti-malaria treatment is right for you. The CDC recommends that all visitors to Colombia get a yellow fever vaccination. Travelers in Bogotá without their shots can go to the long-distance bus terminal, where a medical clinic will administer shots for anyone, including foreigners, for free.

and Peru. There are no roads linking Leticia to any other city or town in the country, which means to get there you have to fly, or take a boat from Peru or Brazil.

Planning your Amazon adventure

You'll want to make **Leticia** your base of operations, and organize all excursions from there.

Average high temperatures here hover in the 87°F (31°F) range, with humidity typically in the 60–90 percent range. It's also worth noting that there isn't a rainy or dry season in Amazonas, but rather a high-water season and a low-water season on the Amazon. The high season is from December to May and the low season is from June to November.

Arriving in Leticia

Anyone arriving in Leticia is subject to an entrance tax, which is around US$10. There's a **tourist information point** (daily 7am–noon, 2–5pm) in the airport baggage claim next to the entrance-tax payment kiosk. In town you'll encounter tour providers hustling for customers. Many of them run acceptable tours; however, it's best to arrange a tour through the

⊙ TRAVELING TO BRAZIL AND PERU

There's no immigration control between Leticia and Tabatinga, which is the Brazilian town that borders Leticia to the east. As a result, visitors can travel freely between the two municipalities. However, those who wish to venture deeper into Brazil or Peru will first need to get an exit stamp in Leticia. This can be done at the immigration office in the airport (daily 8am–5pm). You then have 24 hours to exit the country.

reputable companies listed in this book, or through your hostel or hotel. Know that due to Leticia's remote locale, Wi-fi in many hostels and hotels isn't exactly lightning fast.

Around town

At the start of Leticia's downtown, at Calle 8 and Carrera 11, you'll find **Parque Orellana**. There's a large amphitheater in the center, which often

Squirrel monkey on Isla de Los Micos

hosts outdoor concerts on weekends. If you head a block west from the park on Calle 8 you'll reach the *muelle* (dock), the disembarking and departure point for all boats coming to and from town. Its adjacent waterfront walkway is known as the **Malecón Turistico**, a type of promenade. Anyone booking an excursion to anywhere else on the Amazon will leave from this area.

Just above the docks you'll find the **mercado municipal** (local market; Mon–Sat 4am–7pm, Sun 4am–2pm), which is another in Latin America's great tradition of indoor and open-air municipal produce markets. Two blocks north on Carrera 11 is Parque Santander, which is the town's main plaza. Every night at sundown it's possible to climb up to the top of the bell tower in La Catedral, the cathedral on the east side of the park (US$1 to climb up). From here you'll witness the return of hundreds, if not thousands, of green macaws to their homes in the park's trees. It's also offers amazing views of the Amazonian frontier

ISLA DE LOS MICOS

35km (22 miles) northwest of Leticia, lies **Isla de Los Micos** ㊾, a small island overrun by the *mico fraile* (squirrel monkey). The island is more a tourist attraction than a protected area, with visitors following professional guides around marked pathways and feeding banana pieces (the only food allowed) to the ravenous inhabitants. The friendly primates are not afraid of human contact, which makes for great photo-ops, but be sure to keep your pockets zipped up and any small valuables out of reach of the thieving critters. Many tour operators bundle a trip to this island in their package price, but you can go on your own via water taxi (US$5 each way) and pay the US$10 entry fee yourself.

PUERTO NARIÑO

Puerto Nariño ㊿ is fast becoming one of the most popular outposts on the Amazon River – a trend that has its positives and negatives. The community itself is an ideal to aspire to: some 1,200 people (many of them members of the 22 indigenous communities that live in the surrounding areas) have created the smallest official settlement in Colombian Amazonia, and it runs like a dream. There are no cars in Puerto Nariño, and the only vehicle is a tractor used for garbage collection. How Puerto Nariño evolves in the future will be interesting to see, considering it is a young settlement (founded in 1961), with limitless potential.

The only way to arrive here is by boat (US$10 each way from Leticia; first boat at 8am and last at 3.30pm). You'll arrive at the long dock at the town's entrance, and the first thing you'll notice is that everything is built on stilts, which is a safeguard for the high-water season. Getting lost isn't an issue in Puerto Nariño,

PUERTO NARIÑO

as the town is only about four square blocks. In the center you'll find kiosks selling beer, *pinchos,* and grilled river fish, as well as one of the town's two restaurants. Fish is the best option, but be sure to ensure that any threatened species, such as *pirarucu*, is in season before ordering.

Excursions from Puerto Nariño

To fully experience the area surrounding Puerto Nariño, book a multi-day stay (three or four nights; best done from Leticia). These often involves a number of activities, including jungle night treks, caiman 'hunts,' (which just involves caiman-spotting on the river from a canoe), Amazon River swims, and pink dolphin-spotting. Piranha fishing is another activity, as is a visit to local indigenous communities

The Amazon River, Leticia

Mountain bikers in Pasto

WHAT TO DO

SHOPPING

In the major cities of Colombia you'll find explosions of commerce everywhere. In Medellín, for example, you can barely throw a rock without hitting a shopping mall of some sort. The downtown areas of the biggest cities tend to offer the best deals, while the zona rosas typically have an abundance of chic boutiques and upscale retailers. Please note that there's a 16% VAT tax on all purchases in Colombia.

In more recent times travelers with an eye for fashion have come to the country on the hunt for knitted purses. The most authentic are typically crafted in indigenous communities, often outside of Valledupar or in Guajira. The quality of these goods is beyond reproach; the elegant method of knitting them has been passed down through generations of indigenous women for hundreds of years. For them it's as much a spiritual act as it is one of crafting. The bags typically range between US$25–30, and this is one time you don't want to haggle. Just pay the asking price and be happy in the knowledge you're getting a quality product for about 75 percent less than what it would cost in a boutique back home.

SHOPPING IN BOGOTÁ

Bogotá's principal shopping district is the Zona Rosa. Here, three shopping malls sit one on top of the other: the **Centro Andino** (Carrera 11, no. 82–71; tel: 1-621 3111; www.centroandino.com.co), which has a Cine Colombia multiplex; **El Retiro** (Calle 81, no. 11–75; tel: 1-745 5545; www.elretirobogota.com), where you can find Andres Carne de Res, Colombia's most mind-boggling theme-restaurant; and **Centro Comercial**

Atlantis (Calle 81, no. 13–05; tel: 1-606 6200; www.atlantis plaza.com), home to American exports like Hard Rock Café and Chuck E. Cheese's.

La Candelaria, especially along Carrera 3, is a great place to browse for handmade jewelry. For artisanal products (artisanias), try **Almacén las Aguas** (Carrera 2, no. 18a-58; tel: 1-284 3095; www.artesaniasdecolombia.com.co), which is run by Artesanias de Colombia. **The Emerald Trade Center** (Avenida Jiménez, no. 5–43) is home to multiple emerald vendors and jewellers that operate over three floors in a building adjacent to La Candelaria, meaning that it's impossible to see every item and bit of jewelry in one stop. All pieces on sale are guaranteed by CDTEC, a joint government-private emerald authenticator, so shoppers can be sure they are scoring authentic jewels. There is also a *casa de cambio* (exchange house) called Millennium, located just inside the entrance to the ETC.

The **flea market** (Mercado de las Pulgas) at Usaquén, held every Sunday, is located around the plaza on Carrera 6a and down through Calle 120 (www.pulgasusaquen.com). Here you'll find various stalls selling art, woodworking, handicrafts, clothing and more.

SHOPPING IN MEDELLÍN

There's no shortage of shopping centers in Medellín. Every district has at least one (often many). Many of the most upscale are found in the El Poblado neighborhood, but good discounts on clothing and goods can be found on and around Avenida Oriental in centro. Some of the most popular *centro comerciales* include **La Strada** (Carrera 43A, no. 1S–50; www.lastrada.com.co), **Santa Fé** (Carrera 43, no. 7s–170; www.centrocomercial santafe.com/medellin) and Premium Plaza in barrio **San Diego** (Carrera 43a at Calle 30; www.ccpremiumplaza.com).

Tourist shops in Cartagena

SHOPPING IN CARTAGENA

Head to **Plaza Santo Domingo**, in the walled city, for expensive antique shops. There are a number of emerald-selling jewelery shops in *centro*. **Plaza de las Bóvedas**, also in the walled city, is great for handicrafts; the **Librería Nacional** (Carrera 7, no. 36-27; tel: 5-664 1448) is a bookshop in the walled city with a great selection. For emeralds, try **Lucy Jewelry** (Calle 35, no. 3-19; tel: 5-664 4255; www.lucyjewelrycartagena.com) located near Plaza Santo Domingo in the walled city.

Elsewhere in the city, check out the **Centro Comercial Getsemaní** (Calle 25, no. 8B-74; tel: 5-664 7085; www.centrocomercialgetsemani.com), a shopping center with a nice selection of artesenias where the convent is located. The **Mercado Bazurto**, on the road towards Cartagena from the bus terminal, is a good, authentic outdoor market featuring plenty of fruits and vegetables as well as meat and fish.

THE ARTS

Colombia has a thriving and diverse arts scene, and there's no shortage of both traditional and contemporary galleries and exhibits to immerse yourself in.

Museo Botero, Bogotà

BOGOTÁ

Dibs by Culture Shock (Carerra 3, no. 11-24; tel: 300-312 2215), a little La Candeleria gallery features works for sale from local and international street artists. If your tastes are a little more traditional, check out **Galeria Alonso Garces** (Carrera 5, no. 26-92; tel: 1-337 5827 www.alonsogarcesgaleria.com), located across the street from Librería Luvina. It features both national and international works and hosts about six exhibitions per year. There's also a store where guests can purchase art and books.

For art buffs and non-art buffs alike, no trip to Bogotá is complete without a visit to the **Museo Botero** (Calle 11, no. 4-21; tel: 1-343 1316; www.banrepcultural.org/museo-botero; Mon-Sat 9am-7pm, Sun and holidays 10am-5pm; closed Tue; last admission a half hour before closing; US$1; guided visits in Spanish multiple times daily). The

Museo Botero features 123 pieces from the famed sculptor Fernando Botero's. They were donated by him to the Banco de la República who converted an old colonial mansion into this museum space. There's also some 85 pieces on display from various international artists. For modern art enthusiasts, head over to the **Museo de arte Moderno** (Calle 24 near Parque de la Independencia; tel: 1-286 0466; www.mambogota.com). Known as MAMBO to locals, the four floors of this comprehensive museum are home to a wide-ranging collection of 20th century artwork and rotating exhibits. There's a permanent collection featuring works by Picasso, Dali and Warhol, among others.

MEDELLÍN

Medellín's premier art gallery is the **Museo de Arte Moderno** (Carrera 44, no. 19a–100; tel: 4-444 2622; www.elmamm.org), and is located north of Poblado and has a collection of photographs and paintings, including those by Déborah Arango. It also has a screening room.

CALI

Cali has a thriving arts and theatre scene. Be sure to check out the **Teatro Aire Libre Los Cristales** (Carrera 14a oeste, no. 6–00; tel: 2-557 6421) whilst in town. The best way to see their upcoming events is on their Facebook page; this amphitheater was built in 1986 and still plays host to various concerts and artistic showings. The **Teatro Experimental** (Calle 7, no. 8–63; tel: 2-884 3820; www.enriquebuenaventura.org) is home to a resident theater group that puts on contemporary productions, in Spanish only. For more traditional productions, try the **Teatro Municipal** (Carrera 5, no. 6–64; tel: 2-881 3131; www.teatromunicipal.gov.co). This theater has been hosting cultural acts since 1918. Here you'll find ballet, opera and classical music concerts.

ADVENTURE SPORTS

Canyoning. Colombia's striking scenery also allows for some truly unique and epic adventure sports such as canyoning, which is essentially abseiling down waterfalls. Canyoning is typically offered on a tour, which includes all the relevant safety equipment, such as helmets, harnesses, ropes, and, of course, guides. Heights vary from waterfall to waterfall, but the Cascadas Juan Curi, near San Gil, is 65 meters (213ft) tall, which, together with the spectacular waterfall, makes it one of the most popular canyoning spots in the country.

Diving. Lest anyone forget, Colombia is the only country in South America to boast both a Pacific and a Caribbean coast, which means that there are plenty of great opportunities for diving here. Many tend to head straight to the Caribbean Coast, where there is an abundance of dive stores in the cities and towns. The islands of San Andrés and Providencia are also very popular. Conditions here are ideal due to the sheer amount of reefs, cays, and coral islands that are found throughout in this part of the Caribbean.

Rafting. San Gil, in Santander Department, is ground zero for river rafting. There are ideal conditions in the mountains at the Fonce and Suárez Rivers. There's still only one reputable company for extreme rafting in San Gil: **Colombia Rafting Expeditions** (https://www.colombiarafting.com/).

Other popular locales for rafting include San Agustín, in Huila Department, Río Negro to Tobia, Cudinamarca, the River Barragan in the Zona Cafetera, the Cauca Valley, San Juan in Antioquia, and Flandes in Tolima Department.

Paragliding. Many travelers may come to San Gil and Bucaramanga for the paragliding, but this is not the only spot in which to enjoy this sport. From Santander to the Cauca Valley, conditions are great for paragliding; not only that, but the breathtaking scenery that defines much of Colombia means many regions are best seen from above. There really is nothing like looking down at Colombia's raw beauty – all those rolling green hills, cloud forests, and canopy jungles – from a few hundred meters up in the air.

Anyone can reserve a tandem flight, and no previous experience or training is necessary. Many people come to Santander to fly over the Chicamocha Canyon, which is the largest in Colombia. Soaring a few hundred meters over this gorge is an experience in itself, and these flights typically last 30–60 minutes. Paragliding tours also operate out of other locations as well, including Medellín and Cali. One of the best areas in the entire country is around the town of Roldanillo, in the Valle de Cauca.

Kitesurfing. Come to the Guajira Peninsula, in particular Cabo de la Vela, and you'll find strong offshore winds that make this an ideal spot for kitesurfing. During the day, the skyline here is peppered with brightly colored canopies while on the surface of the sea happy folks zip along on flat

Wreck diving, off San Andrés Island

boards. Cartagena is also an ideal spot for kitesurfing, and windsurfing.

Mountain biking. Cycling is one of Colombia's most popular sports, which means that there are plenty of opportunities to cycle throughout the country, with mountain biking being one of the more popular means of travel. This is due to Colombia's mountainous terrain, which not only gives mountain bikers quite a workout, but also provides beautiful scenery scarcely rivalled throughout the world.

Many head to Santander and cycle the mountains around San Gil and the Chicamocha Canyon. There are also great conditions outside of Bogotá in Boyacá, as well as in and around Medellín. In San Gil the best company for reserving a tour and renting bikes is Colombian Bike Junkies.

Ziplining through the Chicamocha Canyon

thick tree canopy. Colombia is rife with these ideal conditions, and not only are there canopy tours in lush hilly areas like those outside Medellín, but there are also tours over water in the Reserva Río Claro (see page 37). In San Gil, a zipline has been installed that runs a few hundred meters from one side of a canyon to another. The steep drops make for a wild ride.

CHILDREN'S COLOMBIA

Any family flying into Bogotá should make a beeline for **Andres Carne de Res**. This is probably the most-lively steakhouse in the entire country. The original location is a sprawling, 2000-seater hacienda turned restaurant located about 45 minutes north of the country. At night adults party until dawn, but during the day, kids can enjoy face-painting, clowns, a climbing wall, and even dance lessons go with their food. It's a can't-miss experience.

Kids will also enjoy **Divercity** (Avenida Carerra 45 #185 Centro Comercial Santafé; www.parquedivercity.com/colombia/bogota), a virtual village located in the Santafé shopping mall that features ball pits, climbing walls, go-karts, and more. There's also role-playing environments where kids can pretend to be doctors, firefighters, journalists and a host of other careers.

Aside from that, Colombia offers so many natural wonders that the kids will often fall right in line alongside adults as far as activities are concerned. Whether it's visiting the **Isla de los Micos** (Monkey Island), in Amazonas, snorkeling the Caribbean coast in **Parque Tayrona**, or partaking in a carriage ride in Cartagena, kids will have just as much fun as mom and dad.

CALENDAR OF EVENTS

January: Feria de Manizales. In early January the coffee-producing city of Manizales throws a diverse party featuring parades, costumes, live music, tango dancing, stunt shows, and beauty queens.

Hay Festival Cartagena. (www.hayfestival.com/cartagena) This is the Cartagena de India branch of the UK's Hay Festival, which takes place at the end of January and focuses on literature, art, cinema, music, geopolitics, and the environment. The purpose is to promote culture and social responsibility.

Carnival de Pasto. (www.carnavaldepasto.org) The southwestern city of Pasto has its own carnival, which takes place at the end of January or around the beginning of February. Face painting with black grease and white flour signifies the emancipation of slaves, and there are floats and processions.

February and March: Barranquilla Carnival. This is one of the biggest carnival celebrations in South America. People flock to downtown Barranquilla where, four days before Ash Wednesday, parades and dancing lead to copious amounts of partying.

March and April: Semana Santa. The traditional Holy Week is a big event throughout the country. Most cities and towns will feature processions, but the pageantry is particularly notable in places like Popayán.

April: Fiesta Leyenda Vallenata. (www.valledupar.com/festival) The city of Valledupar explodes every year in late April with a four-day party celebrating locally invented vallenato music. During the day crowds gather in Plaza Alfonso Lopez, while at night tens of thousands pack the concert area by the river for more revelry. The festival culminates in an award for best musician.

June: Festival Folclórico y Reinado Nacional de Bambuco. From mid-June to early July the biggest festival in Huila Department takes place in Neiva. There's live music, floats, traditional dances, and many eye-catching dresses and costumes.

August: Feria de Flores. (www.feriadelasfloresmedellin.gov.co) In the 'City of the Eternal Spring,' flowers are always in bloom. Medellín celebrates this every year during the first two weeks of August, when harvesters line the streets carrying great floral displays on their backs. There are also horse shows, concerts, and street parties.

Festival del Viento y de los Cometas. Whatever the windiest August weekend is in in Villa de Leyva, that's when the town holds its famous kite festival. For three days everyone packs the central plaza to display their aerial prowess. Contest involve, among other things, best handmade kite and best practitioner in the kids' division.

September: Jazz al Parque. (www.jazzalparque.gov.co) For a weekend in early to mid-September, local and international musicians descend on Bogotá's parks and treat audience members to various types of jazz, including instrumental and big band.

Fiesta de San Pacho. (http://sanpachobendito.org) Every year in September Chocó Department holds their own carnivalesque celebration, which usually lasts for a couple weeks or more.

November: Independence in Cartagena. The first two weeks in Cartagena see parties celebrating the city being the first to achieve independence from Spain. The event is now linked to the national beauty pageant, which, as the official information states, is held to "unite Colombian regions around the beauty of Colombian women."

Festival Pirarucú de Oro. This festival has been going on since 1987, and takes place in mid-November. It celebrates Amazonian popular music, which has influences in Brazil and Peru as well. Live music and dance is the order of the day.

December: Festival de Luces. On the 7th, 8th, and 9th of December, Villa de Leyva's sprawling central square is lit up with fireworks in order to celebrate the impending Christmas.

Feria de Cali. (www.feriadecali.com). From the 25th to 30th of December, Cali reminds the world why it's synonymous with salsa. There are live music concerts, Paso Fino horse parades, revelry, and, of course, much dancing.

EATING OUT

For a long time Colombian cuisine was overlooked by the global foodie scene. Colombia didn't have sexy standouts like Peru's ceviche, world-class beef like Argentina, or the soulful cauldrons of *feijoada* found in Brazil. Or so people thought. But as the years go on and the country opens up more and more to tourism, people are discovering its myriad culinary delights. The food here is unlike anywhere else on the continent. Although the techniques may change from department to department, the majority of dishes are linked by a common theme: a commitment to quality ingredients and a humble approach to putting them together. The below is a regional breakdown of Colombia's best food and drinks.

WHAT TO EAT IN...

Bogotá

Ajiaco is the star of the show here. Every Bogotá resident eats it, and everyone's mother or grandmother probably has their own special recipe. Essentially it's a chicken stew, made from yucca, maize, various types of potato (including the delicious, golf-ball sized *papas criollas*), and wild *campesino* herbs like *guascas*. It is served with capers, avocados, and crème fraiche. Even in the most traditional restaurants, it is served in an earthen bowl.

There's a certain gastronomic ritual that many Bogátanos adhere to. This is known as 'onces' and it is an afternoon snack eaten around 5pm (despite its name meaning 11) that includes coffee, aromática, or chocolate, plus delectable pastries like *almojabanas* (Colombian cheese bread).

You can also find blood sausage (*morcilla*) and tripe (*chunchullo*) in and around Bogotá. *Caldo de Raíz* (soup of the root), is another staple, and only the most adventurous culinary aficionados need apply. Essentially it's a broth made with chopped up bits of bull penis and testicles, served with avocado. According to folklore the dish is an aphrodisiac, although reliable evidence is yet to transpire. To erase that image, consider one of Bogotá's great desserts: *cuajada con melao*, which is fresh cheese drizzled with dark cane syrup.

Ajiaco

Santander

Head to the colonial town of Barichara and almost right away you'll notice a curious ant (*hormiga*) theme about the town. Not only do the Barichara locals – and those throughout Santander – like to name things after ants, they also like to eat them. *Hormigas culonas* (large-bottomed black ants), are a famous culinary delight in the area. When in season (around Easter), you'll find them in many stores and restaurants. They're surprising delightful, with a crispy, salty taste, similar to peanuts. In keeping with Colombia's obsession with food and sex, locals will tell you this dish has aphrodisiac qualities as well, but again with no discernible proof.

Mute is a corn soup with different types of cereals, and it's sort of the Santander's answer to *ajiaco*. Often it is made with

Mojarra frita with patacones, fried plantain, and rice

beef ribs and pork. You can also find goat served with tripe and intestines throughout Santander, as well as pigeon. In the north exists a delicious dish called *rampuchada*, which is a spicy stew made with fish from the Zulia River. *Hallacas* are meat-filled pockets made from cornmeal that are reminiscent of a Mexican *tamale*, except bigger. *Carne orneada* is dried, salted meat that is not quite as tough as beef jerky, but of a similar texture, marinated in pineapple and unrefined sugarcane. *Bocadillo veleño* is a common sweet made from guava jelly and panela that is also found in other parts of Colombia.

The Caribbean

The order of the day in the Caribbean lowlands is fish. The most common type you'll find here is mojarra, a flaky white fish often fried and served with salad and fried plantains. Another typical side dish is coconut rice (*arroz de coco*), which is perfectly aromatic and best eaten by the sea. *Arroz de mariscos* (seafood rice) or *arroz de camarones* (shrimp rice) are both popular dishes and are typically served as main courses. For street food, one option found in most coastal cities is *ceviche de camarones* (shrimp cocktail). This can throw many visitors, because Colombians don't have the same definition of ceviche as the Peruvians. If you get a *ceviche de camarones*, it is prepared shrimp and or *mariscos* or *pulpo* (shellfish and octopus) made in the typical cocktail style, meaning it is prepared fish mixed with lime juice, ketchup and mayonnaise and served with crackers.

One of the most famous dishes in all of Caribbean Colombia is the *cazuela de mariscos*, a boiling black cauldron of shellfish stew, rich and yellow, with all the flavors of fish, mussels, shrimp, langoustines, and more. *Sancocho de pescado* (fish stew) is an equally delicious soup but much lighter and typically made with just fish. *Chipichipi* (a frontrunner for best name for food ever) is a type of clam found along the coast and served with rice. Of course, *arepas* (cheese and flour patties served on its own or topped with meat) and *empanadas* are popular here as well, as they are in most other parts of the country.

Northwest Colombia

In Antioquia, you are treated to rich, humble food served in ample proportions. This is *campesino* fare: a dish intended to provide sustenance throughout a long workday. Case in point: the heavyweight-sized *bandeja paisa*, a tray loaded with a kaleidoscopic array of meats, including crispy pork skin (*chicharrón*) and sausage, finished off with a fried egg. As if this wasn't enough of an assault, they then load up the side with rice, beans (those from Antioquia are the best), *manioc*, fried plantains, and salad (just to keep it light). This dish has its origins around Medellín, but you can find it in most other parts of the country. Another similar dish is the *calentado paisa*, a kind of hash made from beans, rice, and *carne mechada* (stewed, tender beef), topped with an egg and served with *arepas*. *Natilla* is a circular sponge cake (kind of like a doughnut), that you can see being fried up in the bakeries and street vendors around Medellín. *Salpicón*, a fruit salad topped with crème and syrups, is also ubiquitous here.

Southern Colombia

The most noteworthy aspect of southern Colombian cooking is that, unlike most other parts of the country, it doesn't often use potatoes in its cuisine. Here corn, plantains, rice, and avocado are the staples. You can find many of these ingredients in famed Caleño dishes like *tamales*. Caleño *tamales* are slightly different than those found in other areas, such as Bogotá, as they are often bigger and feature larger portions of meat, although still wrapped in banana leaves. *Manjar blanco* is a popular dessert here, which, like caramel, is made from milk and sugar. *Cuy* (guinea pig), which is also popular in Peru and Ecuador, can be found close to the southern border.

WHAT TO DRINK

Coffee

This is of course a staple of Colombia and one of its principal exports. It will come as a surprise to many that most Colombians drink instant coffee at home, as they often don't have the budget to stock up on gourmet beans. Even more of an eye-opener is the fact that the famous Juan Valdez was never an actual coffee company, but a character created to help sell coffee to other countries. You'll now see Juan Valdez gourmet coffee chains across the country, but even these were a direct response to the popularity of Starbucks (note the suspiciously similar design schemes of Juan Valdez when compared to Starbucks).

The best way to take coffee in Colombia (aside from staying at a coffee finca) is from a street vendor. A *tinto* is a black coffee with sugar, *café con leche* includes milk, and if you want milk on the side you can ask for the *leche aparte*. If you like it strong, ask for *café cargado*.

Aguapanela

Aguapanela is basically what the name implies: *agua* (water) combined with *panela* (unrefined sugarcane). You can drink it hot or cold and the outside temperature will determine which way is best.

Aromática

This is an herbal tea infused with various herbs and fruits. Flavors include *yerba buena*, *manzania*, limonaria, and *canela* (cinnamon). It's a great cold-weather drink and many of the street vendors mix in rum or whiskey, which makes for a tasty Christmastime tipple.

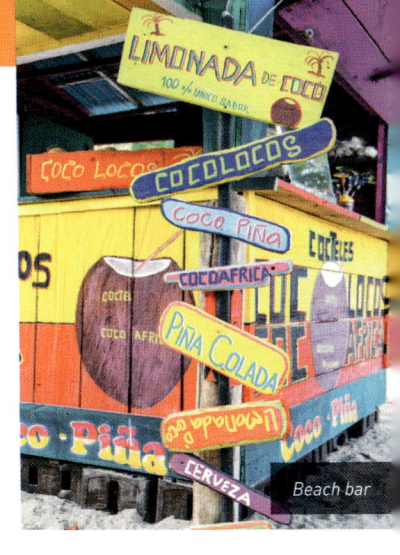

Beach bar

Beer

Where it concerns local beers, most people opt for those brewed by the Bogotá Beer Company, a national brewery and restaurant chain that does a solid lager and some interesting microbrews. You can find this dark-bottled beer in certain restaurants, most large-chain supermarkets, and many hostels.

Chicha

Chicha is a fermented corn liquor that has its roots in the country. It's a *campesino* drink, not terribly strong but incredibly potent. Its thick texture is reminiscent more of chowder than of alcohol, and if you sit down at a *chicheria*, try not to smell it before downing it. There is also a non-alcoholic, sugary, fruit-infused version of *chicha* that has a smoother consistency and makes a great soft drink. You can find it in certain restaurants.

Liquor

Colombia is a drinking country, so teetotalers should know that they may be offered alcohol in local homes. Don't worry though – no one will be offended if you pass. Rum is popular in most areas of the country, as is whiskey. However, those on the coast tend to drink Old Parr. As for rum, Ron Medellín is probably the best brand. And, of course, it's the Paisas from Medellín that made *aguardiente* (an anise-flavored sugarcane liquor sometimes called *guaro*) famous. Spend more than a day or two in the city and the stuff will flow like water.

Wine is quite expensive in Colombia and you'll find the selection rather limited in many markets.

Fruit juice

Colombians love fresh fruit juice. Many fruits that flourish in Mediterranean climates, including grapes, apples, and bananas, also thrive here. You aren't likely to find lemons in Colombia; however limes are abundant. Some local fruits include *curuba* (banana passion fruit), *guayaba* (guava), *lulo* (a small orange fruit), *maracuyá* (passion fruit), *mora* (blackberry), *sandia* (watermelon), papaya, *pitahaya* (dragon fruit), and *tomate de árbol* (tree tomato), which is a favorite in Colombian households. Colombians will juice just about anything, but when ordering be warned that they often serve it either *con leche* (with milk) or *solo agua* (just water).

Hot chocolate

You may be surprised to learn that hot chocolate is often drunk at breakfast in Colombia (and this could be a contributing factor as to why the people in Colombia are so happy).

TO HELP YOU ORDER

Do you have a table for...? Tiene una mesa para...?
I have a reservation Tengo una reserva
breakfast/lunch/dinner desayuno/almuerzo/cena
I'm a vegetarian Soy vegetariano(a)
wine list la carta de vinos
What would you recommend? Qué recomienda?

MENU READER

a la plancha grilled
aguacate avocado
ajo garlic
al horno baked
almejas clams
anchoa anchovy
atún tuna
aves poultry
batata sweet potato
berenjena eggplant
calamares squid
camarones shrimp
cabra goat
cebolla onion
cerdo/chancho/puerco pork
chicharrón fried pork belly
chorizo Spanish-style sausage
frambuesa raspberry
fresa strawberry
frito(a) fried
hamburguesa hamburger
champiñones mushrooms

jamón ham
langostinos prawns
lengua tongue
lima lime
limón lemon
lomito tenderloin
mariscos shellfish
morcilla blood sausage
papa potato
pavo turkey
pechuga breast
piernas legs
pitaya dragon fruit
pollo chicken
pomelo grapefruit
porotos beans
puerro leeks
sandía watermelon
sardinas sardines
ternera veal
trucha trout
uvas grapes
vieiras scallops

PLACES TO EAT

Price for a two-course meal for one person, including a glass of wine and service charge.

$$$$	over $50
$$$	$25-50
$$	$10-25
$	$0-10

BOGOTÁ

La Candelaria

Paella de la Candelaria $$ *Calle 11, no. 5–13*. This is the place to come for paella in La Candelaria. Friendly owners and good service. Open for lunch only.

Pita Wok $ *Carrera 4, no. 12c–54; tel: 1-243 7356*; www.pitawok.com. This Middle-Eastern eatery may be little, but it does solid shawarma, wraps and pitas. Both the *lafa* and combo plates are good choices, and there are vegetarian options as well. They also serve fresh juices.

La Puerta $ *Falsa Calle 11, no. 6–50; tel: 1-286 5091*. This tiny Bogotá institution, located just up from Plaza Bolívar, comes highly recommended by locals for its traditional fare, which features humble, hearty dishes such as *ajiaco*, and *tamales*. Be prepared for a long wait at lunchtime.

La Macarena

(It's worth noting that most restaurants in La Macarena operate on similar schedules: closed Mondays and closed between lunch and dinner services.)

Alô Brasil $–$$ *Calle 26c, no. 4–42; tel: 1-243 2564*; www.restaurantealobrasil.com. Almost everyone here, from the owner to the cooks to the servers, is from Brazil. That spells an authentic *Brasilero* dining experience, featuring hits from the north of the country all the way to the south. This includes *bolinha de peixe* (fried fish balls) *bobó de camarao* (shrimp chowder) and various *moquecas* (stews). Best of all they do *feijoada* every weekend. Great ambience too.

La Jugueteria $–$$ *Calle 4a, no. 26d; tel: 1-745 2515;* www.restaurantelajugueteria.com.co. This is a themed restaurant along the lines of Andrés Carne de Res, except even more bizarre (if that's possible). You can dine in a teacup alongside the Incredible Hulk; the menu is mostly *parilla*, heavy on grilled meats.

TaKrai $$ *Calle 26c, no. 4-41; tel: 1-282 7687;* www.facebook.com/takraithaicuisine/. In a narrow, unassuming space local Bogotáno Davíd operates one of the only restaurants featuring authentic Thai recipes (no fusion here) in the city. The menu is mostly a greatest hits of Thai cuisine, with the red and green curries and pad Thai the most popular. This is a good spot for travelers, as Davíd doubles as a server and is happy to speak to his foreign guests in English.

Zona G

Emilia Romagna $$ *Calle 69a, no. 5-32; tel: 1-346 2620;* www.emiliaromagnarestaurante.com. The ambiance of this Zona G Italian eatery is all but perfect – a warm, inviting and soft-lit dining room (with wine bottles wall to wall) leads to a patio lined with fresh greenery. The menu is extensive, covering Mediterranean and regional favorites like gnocchi and veal Milanese, as well as long lists of antipasti and pastas.

Rafael $$ *Calle 70, no. 4-63; tel: 1-255 4138.* Peruvian celebrity chef Rafael Osterling made a name for himself with restaurants in Lima, and now he's brought his operation to Bogotá. Popular dishes like seafood and ceviche are served in elegant surroundings with white-tablecloth dining. Of course you'll want to drink a *pisco sour* with your meal.

Zona Rosa

Andres Carne de Res $$–$$$ *Calle 82, no. 12–21 (located in the El Retiro shopping center); tel: 1-863 7880; www.andrescarnederes.com.* Locals positively revere this themed restaurant, which is located in the heart of the Zona T. It is certainly unique. The restaurant stretches over four floors, each of which has been designated a spiritual moniker: the top floor is *cielo* (heaven), the third is *tierra* (earth), the second is *purgatorio* (purgatory), and the ground floor is *infierno*, which I'm sure you can guess. The menu is *parilla criollo*, or Colombian-style grill. That means sizzling platters of meat and potatoes piled high, cooked to perfection.

Watakushi $$–$$$ *Carrera 12, no. 83-17; tel: 1-218 0743; www.watakushi.com.co.* The staff at this establishment says they serve the best sushi in Bogotá, and they could very well be right. It certainly looks the part, with a modern design in an urban space with a brick exterior. The alluring aroma and rows of signature *sake* bottles tempt you as you come in. Also features Thai dishes.

Villa de Leyva

Artesia $$–$ *Calle 13, no. 9-82; tel: 1-6621 198.* Peruvian/Italian fusion is the name of the game at this restaurant overlooking the Plaza Mayor. They're known for traditional ceviche and lasagna, but their menu extends to pizza and steak dishes as well. Be sure to try the *chicha morada*, a non-alcoholic version of the famous *campesino* fermented corn drink. This one has a refreshingly sweet taste perfect on a hot day in the plaza.

Savia $$–$ *Carrera 9, no. 11–75; tel: 8-474 9859; www.restaurante-savia.com.* Savia is a little hard to find as it's located at the very back of Casa Quintero, an indoor gallery on the northeast corner of Plaza Mayor. The restaurant looks the part; it is situated off a tranquil courtyard featuring a polished yet rustic décor. They serve fish and beef dishes, but this is a good option for vegetarians as it has a good selection of meat free dishes, including tortillas and veggie plates.

MEDELLÍN

Dharma Vegan Resto $ *Carrera 43b, no. 8–31; tel: 4-506 6591.* This vegan option opened in 2016 and is located just off Parque Poblado. The menu is limited; the lunchtime menu is set and the dinner menu features a few main courses along the lines of falafel, burgers and burritos. Everything is vegan here, including the tasty desserts.

Tabun $$ *Carrera 33, no. 7–99; tel: 4-311-8209; www.eltabun.com.* It's nice to have some diversity of eating options in Medellín, and Tabun rounds it out with a variety of Middle Eastern dishes. There's shawarma, hummus, kebabs and even Indian plates like masalas.

Tipicos $ *Carrera 36, no. 10–30; tel: 448 5013; www.facebook.com/3Tipicos/.* There's nothing flashy about this quaint Poblado eatery (in fact it's sandwiched in between trendier restaurants). But it does great, no-frills Antioquian food that will fuel you for an entire day. The *cazuelas* with *frilojes Antioqueños* (beans) are not to be missed.

Viva Italia! $$–$ *Carrera 43b, no. 11–88; tel: 4-266 4699; www.vivaitaliamedellin.com.* Thick-crust fans go someplace else – this is thin, crispy pie all the way. The pepperoni is great; it's probably, overall, the best pizza in Medellín. The restaurant also serves pasta dishes.

ANTIOQUIA
Guatape

La Piedra $$–$ *El Peñol; tel: 311-309 3161.* This eatery is located at the base of El Peñol among other similar restaurants. However, this one has a nice view overlooking the water and an open-air kitchen where you can watch the grill man work his magic. The menu of meat and river fish is vast; try the breaded bass.

Santa fe de Antioquia

Café Don Roberto $-$$ *Calle 10, no. 7–37; tel: 4-853 2294.* This restaurant has a simple menu of standard dishes, like the *bandeja paisa* and the *sancocho de bagre* (catfish). There's also fast food and delicious juices. Best of all there's a pool out back you can cool off in for an extra fee.

Jardín

Bon Apétit $-$$ *Carrera 4, no. 8–10; tel: 301-780 740.* This is a small eatery run by a Colombian-born Russian by way of Asia and Europe. The menu reflects this in that there are a number of great Italian pasta and ramen options on the menu. Try the carbonara.

Las Margaritas $ *Carrera 3, no. 9–68; tel: 311 635 5831.* This restaurant on the plaza does good, standard Antioquian fare like beans, grilled meats and the *bandeja paisa*. Good juices too. The staff are friendly.

ZONA CAFETERA
Pereira

Mediterráneo $-$$ *Avenida Circunvalar, no. 4-47; tel: 6-331 0398; see facebook.* This is a popular spot with locals. The restaurant serves steaks, crepes, seafood, fondus, and a many other things among the pleasant atmosphere on the terrace.

Manizales

El Zaguán $-$$ *Paisa Carrera 23, no. 31–27.* This restaurant in centro is reasonably priced and cosy. You enter through a long bamboo corridor and dine on dishes like the typical *bandeja paisa*. There's also a set-lunch menu.

Spago $$ *Calle 59, no. 24a-06; tel: 6-885 3328;* www.spagorestaurante.com. Spago is located east of the center and does some very tasty Italian food. The locals seem to agree. They serve a great variety of pastas.

SANTANDER
Bucamaranga

El Viejo Chiflas $$ *Carrera 33, no. 34–10; tel: 7-632 0640;* www.elviejochiflasrestaurante.inf.travel. This is a quality local spot in the heart of Buca's Zona Rosa. They do a lot of comfort food and grilled meats. Try the *cabrito* (goat).

Mercagán $$ *Parque San Pio; tel: 643 5630;* www.mercaganparrilla.com. Many claim this restaurant (one of a chain, this one at Parque San Pio) to be the best steak in Colombia. That's up for debate, but it does do solid beef in expansive chophouse surroundings. It also does good salads. Go right for the *lomo fino*.

Barichara

Las Cruces $$–$ *Carrera 5, no. 4–26; tel: 726 7577.* This restaurant is located in the Foundacaion Escuela Taller Barichara. The menu items here are more refined and served around a lush central courtyard. Local delicacies include beef in *hormiga* sauce (yup, ants). Open Daily December through January; on weekends only during low season.

Pizzeria 7 Tigres $$–$ *Carrera 6, no. 10–24; tel: 312-521 9962.* The best pizza in town is at this unique little joint complete with funky patio seating on a rolling green hill. The menu isn't big, but it certainly packs a punch: delicious thin-crust pizzas with unique toppings like chicken marinated in Middle-Eastern spices. Pita bread, salads and desserts are also available. Good *limonadas*; the Chilean cabernet is good too.

CARTAGENA
Getsemaní

Saint Roque $$–$ *Calle Espiritu Santo 10c, no. 29–214; tel: 316 477 7429.* Saint Roque bills itself as the only Indonesian restaurant in the country. It's certainly the only such option in Cartagena. The menu contains recipes passed down from the chef's Indonesian mother, like chicken sates and lagoustines pepesan. The restaurant also works with the La Vecina foundation (www.lavecina.org), which helps underprivileged children in Cartagena.

The walled city

Donjuán $$$ *Calle del Colegio, no. 34-60; tel 5-664 3857; www.donjuan-cartagena.com.* This is another restaurant that wins the décor game. The style here is "Caribbean bistro," done up in a bright dining room with black-and-white tiled floors. While the menu is heavy on fish, there's good diversity in the form of steaks, risotto, pastas and pork dishes.

La Mulata $ *Calle Quero, no. 9-58; www.lamulatacartagena.blogspot.com.co.* This is a popular lunchtime spot that does solid Caribbean food with some other plates thrown in for good measure, like BBQ ribs. There are set lunch specials but anything with fish or seafood is the way to go (try the seafood casserole). Usually has a vegetarian option.

San Diego

Carmen $$$ *Calle Del Santisimo, no. 8-19; tel: 5-664 5116; www.carmencartagena.com.* It's easy to let Carmen's ambiance (the main dining area is in beautifully lit courtyard complete with palms) put you under its spell. And the contemporary cuisine on offer only adds to the experience. Refined plates featuring staples like octopus, Caribbean fish and shrimp are on the menu, as are some unique standouts like confit of duck.

La Cevecheria $$ *Calle Stuart 714; tel: 5-660 1492; www.lacevicheriacartagena.com.* This is one of the highest ranked eateries in the San Diego quarter. You'll realize the hype is justified before you even sit down, as platters of freshly grilled seafood and citrusy ceviches make their way around the dining room. On top of every fish and shellfish under the sun, La Cevecheria has a great list of cocktails.

CALI

San Antonio and the west

Teatro Mágico del Sabor $$$ *Calle 4, no. 10–30; tel: 892 2254; www.teatromagicodelsabor.com.* The open-air kitchen offers guests dinner and a show. The menu is mainly local fare like fish and steak, all exquisitely prepared. Here the chef is the center of attention, but people come for the overall communal vibe.

El Buen Alimento Alquimia Vegetariana $$$ *Calle 2, no. 4–53; tel: 2-375 5738; www.elbuenalimento.com.* "Alchemy" is in the name, and that's a bit of what this option does. They get creative with veggie twists on classic meat dishes, like burgers and mixed *parillas* featuring soy sausage and ham. Also sushi, wraps and falafel.

North and east Cali

FARO Granada $$ *Avenida 9N, no. 12–76; tel: 2-667 6786.* This is another institution in Cali. They serve wild artistic plates of Mediterranean/Peruvian fusion. They also play live music.

Pampero $$ *Calle 21N, no. 9–12; tel: 2-661 3117; www.pamperoparrilla.com.* Downright amazing Argentine steaks. It's nice to sit in the open air and enjoy a *bife de chorizo*. Good empanadas too.

A–Z TRAVEL TIPS

A SUMMARY OF PRACTICAL INFORMATION

- **A** Accommodation 115
  - Addresses 115
  - Airports 116
- **B** Budgeting for your trip 116
- **C** Car rental 117
  - Children 117
  - Climate 118
  - Crime and safety 118
  - Customs 119
- **D** Disabled travelers 119
- **E** Electricity 120
  - Embassies and consulates 120
  - Emergency numbers 120
- **G** Getting there 121
- **H** Health and medical care 122
- **L** Left luggage 124
  - LGBTQ travelers 124
- **M** Media 124
  - Money 125
- **N** Nightlife 125
- **O** Opening hours 126
- **P** Postal services 126
  - Public holidays 126
- **R** Religious services 127
  - Restrooms 127
- **S** Smoking 128
- **T** Tax 128
  - Telephones 128
  - Time zone 129
  - Tipping 129
  - Tourist information 129
  - Tour operators 130
  - Transport 130
- **V** Visas 132
- **W** Weights and measures 133
  - Women travelers 133

ACCOMMODATION

Hostel prices tend to be comparable throughout the country, while hotels range from low to mid-range and high end. Outside of cities and towns you can sometimes find fincas (farmhouses) that have been converted into guesthouses, similar to a bed-and-breakfast. Usually this involves sharing space with the owner(s) of the finca (often a family), and breakfast is typically included. The same is true of hospedajes (often converted homes run by a family). Those visiting the Zona Cafetera can choose to stay on a working coffee farm, which is experience in itself and highly recommended.

ADDRESSES

Colombia's address system can throw anyone off. It is similar to many other countries in South America. It works like this: street-crossing-house number. Or, using a real-life example, you'll likely encounter: Carrera 11, no. 15–23.

Calles and carreras are streets and avenues, and they are typically numbered. In this instance 15 would be a calle. In Colombian addresses, typically Carreras cross calles and vice-versa. You are just as likely to see an address like 'Carrera 11, no. 15–23' as you are 'Calle 15, no. 11–23'. Which comes first depends on which block the building faces. The final field represents the building or house number.

> I'd like a room with twin beds/double bed **Quisiera una habitación con dos camas/cama matrimonial**
> What's the price? **¿Cuál es el precio?**
> Is breakfast included? **¿El desayuno está incluído?**
> Is there a private homestay near here? **¿Conoce una casa particular por aquí?**

AIRPORTS (SEE GETTING THERE)

Most international travelers will be flying into **Aeropuerto Internacional El Dorado** (BOG; Calle 26, 1103–9; tel 1-266 2000; www.eldorado.aero), which is located 13km (8 miles) northeast of Bogotá's city center. The airport underwent a full renovation and upgrade in 2012, adding a second terminal to the structure. It is now comprised of terminal 1 (domestic and international flights) and terminal 2 (formerly known as *Puenté Aereo*, which is operated by Avianca and offers domestic flights only).

The other international airports in Colombia are Cartagena's **Rafael Núñez International** (tel: 5-656 9200; www.sacsa.com.co), Medellín's **José María Córdova International** (tel: 4-402 5110; www.aeropuertojosemariacordova.com), Cali's **Alfonso Bonilla Aragón** (tel: 2-280 1515; www.aerocali.com.co), and Barranquilla's **Ernesto Cortissoz International** (tel: 5-316 0900). Other airports that also receive international flights include San Andrés' **Gustavo Rojas Pinilla International** (tel: 8-512 0020) and Pereira's **Matecaña International** (tel: 6-314 8151).

B

BUDGETING FOR YOUR TRIP

Average prices when traveling around Colombia:
Beer: US$1.50
Glass of house wine: US$ 2.50
Main course at budget restaurant: US$3
Main course at a moderate restaurant: US$5–8
Main course at an expensive restaurant: US$10+
Reservation at a cheap hotel: US$15–25 per night
Reservation at a moderate hotel: US$25–60 per night
Reservation at an expensive hotel: US$80+
Average taxi fare around most large cities: US$5–8
Average taxi fare around smaller cities and towns: US$2–5

Average price of a city bus ticket: US$0.75
Average price for a metro ticket: US$0.75

C

CAR RENTAL (SEE TRANSPORT)

All in all, the interconnected nature of Colombia means road trips are a great way to see a country filled with stunning natural landscapes. Most visitors will likely be renting their vehicles, and there are good deals on economy-size cars averaging around US$30–40 per day (often better deals can be found on fare aggregator websites like www.kayak.com and www.rentalcars.com). However, a mid-size vehicle isn't always the best option for traversing some of Colombia's more rugged topography. For mountain and jungle journeys, a four-wheel drive vehicle with high ground clearance is ideal, and these often cost over US$100 per day to rent. Various car rental agencies can be found at most airports in Colombia, as well as throughout major cities and towns. They will require the renter to present a passport and driver's license, and often a credit-card deposit is needed to complete the transaction. Basic car insurance likely won't cover natural damage, such as flooding, so it's always best for those thinking about going on a country road trip to inquire about extra coverage.

CHILDREN

Like many Latin American countries, Colombia has a family-oriented culture. Often hotels and other establishments will make accommodations for children, and kids usually receive reduced-price admission at places like museums and theme parks, provided they are aged under 12 or thereabouts. Often children under three can receive free or reduced-fare bus and airline tickets if they share a seat with a parent. Many of the higher end hotels offer baby-sitting services, but finding this in mid-range and budget lodgings isn't likely.

CLIMATE

Due to Colombia's position near the equator, it doesn't enjoy seasons in the strictest sense of the word. Temperature variations in the country depend on location and altitude: the coast is always hot and humid; Bogotá is mostly drizzly, overcast, and chilly during the nights. The higher (or lower) you travel in terms of altitude determines the various climates you'll experience. Wet and dry seasons exist in most areas of the country, with precipitation levels varying between locations.

	J	F	M	A	M	J	J	A	S	O	N	D
°C	23	24	24	24	24	24	24	24	24	24	24	23
°F	74	75	76	76	76	76	76	76	76	75	75	74

CRIME AND SAFETY

As of 2018, the government is still working on a tenuous peace with the remaining guerrilla groups in the country. That aside, Colombia is regarded as a generally safe destination for tourists. Tens of thousands of US citizens visit the country every year without incident. However, risks and petty crime do exist here. There have been reports of foreign travelers being mugged or even robbed at gunpoint. Always travel in clearly marked taxis, avoid areas in large cities that are dangerous at night, such as public parks and the downtown neighborhoods, and take the usual precautions: don't leave valuables lying around your hotel or hostel room, avoid wearing flashy jewelry and general displays of wealth. If a member of the police or

> I want to report a theft. **Quiero denunciar un robo.**
> my wallet/handbag/passport **mi cartera/bolso/pasaporte**
> safe (deposit box) **caja fuerte**

military approaches you and asks for ID, always be polite and produce it for them. A paper copy will often suffice.

CUSTOMS

Customs checks occur at airports and land and river crossings between Venezuela, Brazil, Ecuador, and Peru. Due to the drug trade, customs checks at airports can be extensive, and sometimes there are military checks on long-distance bus routes where passengers are asked to produce ID. Always monitor your baggage at airports and bus terminals, and never carry firearms or drugs when traveling.

When entering and exiting Colombia, travelers are allowed the following: 200 cigarettes, 50 cigars, and fewer than 50 grams of tobacco; two bottles of alcoholic beverages; and a reasonable quantity of perfume. Currency import regulations state that amounts exceeding US$10,000 or equivalent currency must be declared on arrival. All vegetables, plants and food of animal origin is prohibited from entering or leaving the country.

D

DISABLED TRAVELERS

Disabled travelers to Colombia will find a country that, in some areas, accommodates their needs, yet is woefully underdeveloped in parts. For example, new hotels and lodging options are required to provide disability access, and most live up to this standard. However, in certain older neighborhoods and towns, especially the colonial ones, old buildings and streets may not be suitable for disabled travelers. As for transportation, the modern metro systems in the big cities offer disability access, but local minibuses are typically small and unmodified, which may present problems to mobility-impaired travelers who want to travel to certain local areas.

Some useful online resources include: European Network for Accessible Tourism (ENAT; www.accessibletourism.org), the US State

Department's Traveling with Disabilities section (www.travel.state.gov/content/passports/en/go/disabilities.html), Accessible Journeys (www.disabilitytravel.com/access-network), and the Society for Accessible Travel & Hospitality's list of disability travel websites (www.sath.org/disability-travel-websites).

E

ELECTRICITY

Colombia's voltage is 110V–120V, which is the same as in the US and Canada. Primary socket types are North American grounded or non-grounded (two/three-pin plugs). European plugs will require a plug adapter; 220–240V appliances will require a transformer.

> What's the voltage? **¿Cuál es el voltaje?**
> adaptor/a battery **un adaptador/una pila**

EMBASSIES AND CONSULATES

Canada: Carrera 7, no. 114-33 14th floor; Bogotá; tel: 1-657 9800; www.canadainternational.gc.ca; Mon–Thu 8am–12.30pm, 1.30–5pm, Fri 8am–1.30pm

United Kingdom: Carrera 9, no. 76-49 8th floor; Bogotá; tel: 1-326 8300; www.gov.uk; Mon, Tue, Thu, Fri 9am–12.30pm

United States: Calle 24, no. 48-50, Bogotá; tel: 1-275 2000; https://bogota.usembassy.gov; Mon–Fri 8am–noon

For a full list of embassies visit www.cancilleria.gov.co.

EMERGENCY NUMBERS

National police/Red Cross ambulance 24-hour line/fire department: tel: 123; civil defense: tel: 1-700 6465 (Bogotá), tel: 123 rest of country; tourist police: tel: 1-337 4413 (Bogotá).

GETTING THERE (SEE AIRPORTS)

By air. United Airlines (www.united.com) offers direct once-daily flights from New York, and twice-daily flights from Houston to Bogotá. American Airlines (www.aa.com) also flies direct daily from Miami and Dallas to Bogotá, with other direct flights from Miami to Cali and Medellín Delta (www.delta.com) offer daily flights from Atlanta to Bogotá and sporadic flights from Atlanta to Cartagena Budget carriers Jet Blue (www.jetblue.com) and Spirit Airlines (www.spirit.com) fly direct daily from Fort Lauderdale to Bogotá, Cartagena, and Medellín.Colombian national carrier Avianca (www.avianca.com) offers direct flights from New York to Bogotá, Medellín, and Cartagena, as well as weekly flights from Los Angeles to Bogotá.

There are direct flights weekly from Paris to Bogotá with Air France (www.airfrance.com). There are also weekly flights from Frankfurt with Lufthansa (www.lufthansa.com). There are daily flights from Madrid to Bogotá with Iberia Airlines (www.iberia.com), Air Europa (www.aireuropa.com) and Avianca. Iberia and Avianca also fly a couple times a week direct from Madrid to Medellín, and Avianca flies once a week direct from Madrid to Cali. KLM Royal Dutch Airlines (www.klm.com) offers a few direct flights per week from Amsterdam to Bogotá. For many years travelers from the UK had to change planes in Europe or the US. However, Avianca (www.avianca.com) now offers direct flights from London to

By river. In Amazonas Department, Colombia shares a border with Peru and Brazil at Leticia. Iquitos located 365km (226 miles) to the west of Leticia, is reachable by either speedboat or slow boat. The fast boats are small, cramped, and often poorly ventilated, but they get you there in eight hours (US$85 from Leticia to Iquitos, leaves Tuesday and Sunday). The slow boats take about three days to make the journey; if you have the time, they are by far the better choice (Around US$25, including meals).

There are fast boats from Leticia to Manaus, Brazil, leaving Tuesday, Thursday and Saturday and cost US$173. Also slow boats take seven nights and cost around US$110. All meals are included.

By sea. One of the most popular international trips you can embark on from Colombia is the journey from Cartagena to Panama City by sailboat. This started out as pleasure-boat captains simply trying to earn an extra dollar by ferrying travelers back and forth between countries, and has now become a popular industry. One dependable option is Sailing Koala (www.sailingkoala.com), which not only stops in the San Blas Archipelago, but also arranges dinner with an indigenous Kuna family. Another option is Blue Sailing (www.bluesailing.net). Most boats charge around US$550 for the charter, and food is included. The trip itself takes about five days and passes through the San Blas Archipelago.

By road. There are a few overland routes into Colombia from other countries. These include the southern Colombia–Ecuador crossing at Ipiales–Rumichaca. The main Colombian–Venezuelan crossings are at Cúcuta–San Antonio and, from Maracaibo at Maicao–Paraguachón. However, due to Venezuela's ongoing economic crises, there's high likelihood of border crossings between the two countries being restricted or even prohibited.

H

HEALTH AND MEDICAL CARE (SEE EMERGENCIES)

Before you go

It's recommended that anyone planning a trip to Colombia see their healthcare provider at least six weeks before arriving in the country. It's also helpful to check www.nc.cdc.gov/travel/destinations/traveler/none/Colombia for up-to-date information regarding vaccinations and health concerns in Colombia.

Vaccinations and health risks

Travelers should be up-to-date on routine vaccinations, which include measles, diphtheria, polio, chicken pox, and a yearly flu shot.

HEALTH AND MEDICAL CARE

Anyone planning a trip to the Amazon will want to get a yellow fever vaccination, and these are offered free of charge at the clinic in the Bogotá bus terminal.

Most visitors to Colombia rarely experience any health issues. Typically tap water in the big cities is safe, but many travelers opt for bottled water regardless. Altitude sickness can be a problem for those arriving in the capital, in which case the best prescription is to take it easy and drink plenty of water. Malaria isn't typically a problem in Colombia, however there is a minor risk. Consult your physician in regards to malaria tablets or taking a round of doxycycline.

Insurance

All visitors to Colombia should buy travel insurance before arriving. One helpful resource that can cut through much of the noise and help you to find a good option quick is www.toptenreviews.com/services/insurance/best-travel-insurance/. Make sure the insurance covers all activities you may be partaking in upon arrival, including and especially adventure sports, trekking, and mountaineering. Ensure that your coverage includes air-ambulance service and emergency flights home.

Those who end up in hospital without health insurance will be faced with exorbitant fees. Be sure to get itemized receipts for any medical services you receive.

Pharmacies and hospitals

Pharmacies are common in every city and town in Colombia. Like in many Latin American countries, pharmacists are allowed to dispense basic, non-opioid medications without a prescription. That means visitors suffering from common afflictions (earache, sore throat, traveler's

---

I'm sick. **Estoy enfermo(a)**.
Where's the nearest hospital? **¿Dónde está el hospital más cercano?**
Call a doctor/dentist. **Llame a un médico/dentista.**

diarrhoea, etc) should be able to consult a pharmacist and receive the appropriate medication without paying for a doctor's visit.

As for hospitals, Colombia boasts some of the best on the continent. Travelers' insurance should cover stays in these facilities.

L

LEFT LUGGAGE

Most airport hubs and major bus terminals have left-luggage amenities. Prices vary, but you can expect to pay about US$0.50–1 per hour.

LGBTQ TRAVELERS

For a predominantly Catholic country, Colombia is fairly progressive where it concerns gay rights. It may not have been the first South American country to legalize gay marriage (that honor goes to Argentina), but in 2016 it did become the fourth after a constitutional court extended marriage rights beyond mere civil partnerships. The country's capital city even has a thriving gay neighborhood, Chapinero, with an official LGBT community center (Calle 66, no. 9a–28; tel: 1-249 0049; http://ccdlgbt.blogspot.com.co).

Aside from progressive laws and pockets of gay neighborhoods in major cities, the general culture of Colombia still errs on the traditional side. Homosexuality often isn't as accepted in the smaller towns as it is in the big cities. LGBTQ travelers should be aware of these sensibilities and, although it isn't the ideal scenario, act with prudence. That said, visitors will find most Colombians to be accepting of all kinds of people, sexual orientation aside.

M

MEDIA

Magazines and newspapers

One of the best Spanish-language publications is *Semana* (www.semana.com). For English-language, Bogotá's *The City Paper* is hard to beat. It provides great info and equally good reporting.

MONEY

Colombia's official currency is the Colombian peso (COL$). Notes are available in denominations of COL$2,000, COL$5,000, COL$10,000, COL$20,000, COL$50,000 and COL$100,000; the most common coins are the COL$100, COL$200, COL$500 and COL$1,000. Prices given in this book are in US$; at the time of writing, August 2018, US$1 is worth roughly COL$3,000. For up-to-date conversions, use www.xe.com.

Most ATMs accept international debit and credit cards. Those who want to avoid multiple bank fees and international charges should take out as much money as possible at any given time. Banco de Bogotá (www.bancodebogota.com) is a standard ATM that gives out larger amounts (around COL$600,000 per transaction).

Also, EMV (Europay, MasterCard, and Visa) chip technology means it's more secure than ever to use your card when paying for goods and services in Colombia. Be sure to keep reserves of local currency on hand when traveling throughout the country as remote areas of Colombia often have shortages of ATMs.

> May I pay with a credit card? **¿Se puede pagar con tarjeta?**
> How much is that? **¿Cuánto es?**

N

NIGHTLIFE

Colombia's nightlife is as varied as it is raucous. This is a culture that likes to party and imbibe. The younger generation in the cities and big towns often prefer the rage-all-night discos. Many, in places like Cali, will opt for a *salsoteca* where they can swing their hips until the wee hours of the morning. However, salsa dance knows no age limit, and revelers young and old, male and female, pack the near limitless salsa clubs found throughout the country in order to court one another or just let off some steam after a long workday.

O

OPENING HOURS

Business hours in Colombia are often 8am–noon, 2–5pm (or 6pm), with slightly shorter hours on weekends. The two-hour gap is reserved for the siesta, which is practiced in many establishments (although not all of them in the major cities). Banks are typically open Mon–Fri from 9am–3pm or 4pm. Many establishments will be closed on the biggest of public holidays.

P

POSTAL SERVICES

There are two major postal services in Colombia: **Deprisa** (tel: 01-8000 519393; www.deprisa.com), which is run by the national air carrier Avianca and offers cargo shipping, and **4–72** (tel: 01-8000 111210; www.4-72.com.co). Deprisa can be found at major hubs, but 4-72 has offices in many more locations including most cities and towns. It costs around US$0.75–1 to send an international postcard and around US$1–2 to send a letter up to 20 grams via regular mail. DHL and FedEx also operate in Colombia.

PUBLIC HOLIDAYS

Holidays typically fall on a Monday in Colombia, and if the exact date falls outside of that, the holiday is moved up to the following Monday. Public holidays are known as *puentes* (bridges), because they connect the weekend and working days.

1st January: New Year's Day
Early January: *Día de los Reyes Magos* (Three King's Day), or the Epiphany
19th March: Saint Joseph's Day
Holy Week: *Semana Santa* (Easter)

1st May: Labor Day
May: Ascension Day (occurs 29 days after Easter Sunday)
May/ June: Corpus Christi (around two months after Easter Sunday)
29 June: Saint Peter and Saint Paul
June/ July: Sacred Heart (occurs 10 weeks and one day after Easter Sunday)
20 July: Independence Day
7 August: Battle of Boyacá
15 August: Assumption
12 October: Columbus' arrival in America
1 November: All Saints' Day
11 November: Independence of Cartagena
8 December: Immaculate Conception
25 December: Christmas Day

R

RELIGIOUS SERVICES

Roman Catholicism is the dominant religion in Colombia, and it is a pronounced part of the country's culture. However, while most Colombians are Catholic, they are not entirely beholden to Rome: around 75 percent of the population are nominal Catholics, but only 25 percent identify as practicing Catholics. That means there's a great deal of tolerance for other ideas and lifestyles, with most Colombians adopting a live-and-let-live attitude. In general Colombians observe most religious holidays.

RESTROOMS

Most restrooms in Colombia are of the standard variety. You'll find that, aside from some of the highest-end hotels, you're required to dispose of toilet paper in a bin as opposed to flushing it. If you're not a patron, budget restaurants will often let you use their restrooms for a price, around US$0.20 or so. Most bus terminals charge to use the restrooms.

S

SMOKING

Colombia, like most Latin American countries, has more or less kept up with global trends where it concerns smoking cigarettes. That means there are few areas anymore where you're free to smoke around others. Smoking has been banned indoors and in restaurants, and this goes for the smallest of provincial, family-run eateries as well. Smoking is often allowed on restaurant patios, but not in enclosed public spaces. It goes without saying that if you are invited into someone's home, you should ask before lighting up.

T

TAX

As of 2018 the airport departure tax from Colombia is US$38, and this is not included in your airline ticket. Value Added Tax (VAT) in Colombia is 16 percent. In theory foreigners shouldn't have to pay it, but some more expensive hotels add it on anyway. You can request an official VAT report on your bill from hotels that do add the tax.

TELEPHONES

Most cities and towns have an abundance of telecommunications offices where you can enter a *cabina* (cabin) and make local or international calls, paying by the minute. A screen on the phone often displays the price, and these can vary from location to location. Street vendors with signs marked *minutos* will also allow you to make a call for a charge. You can buy a pay-as-you-go SIM card (around US$2) for your mobile if you choose to make calls within the country, and the main telecommunications carriers are Claro and Movistar. However, these days most Colombians use the cellphone app **WhatsApp** (www.whatsapp.com) to communicate with one another. It's free and allows you to send texts where you are without the need to change SIM cards. Often hotels, *hospedajes,* and hostels will have a WhatsApp number. For making calls, if outside the area you are calling, dial the one-digit area code followed by the seven-digit number.

> I'd like to make a telephone call ... **Quisiera hacer una llamada ...**
> to England/Canada/ United States. **a Inglaterra/Canadá/los Estados Unidos.**
> reverse-charge call **cobro revertido**
> Can you get me this number in ... ? **¿Puede comunicarme con este número en ... ?**

TIME ZONE

GMT-5 throughout the year – meaning it's always five hours earlier than Greenwich Mean Time, one hour behind New York City, and two hours ahead of Los Angeles.

Los Angeles	**Colombia**	New York	London
10am	**noon**	1pm	5pm

TIPPING

A 10 percent gratuity is expected at most sit-down restaurants and cafés. About half of all eateries in Colombia will automatically add a 10-percent gratuity to the bill. Be sure to ask your server before paying if *servicio* is included in the bill or not.

TOURIST INFORMATION

You'll find contact information for the principal tourist offices in each town or city throughout the text. Not every town or city has a functional tourist office, but with tourism on the rise in Colombia, expect this to change in the coming years. The main tourist office in Bogotá is in Plaza Bolívar at Carrera 8, no. 9-83, Mon–Sat 8am–6pm, Sun 8am–4pm.

TOUR OPERATORS

UK and Australia
Insight Guides tel: 020 7403 0284 www.insightguides.com
Exodus Travels tel: 0203 131 5501 www.exodus.co.uk
Intrepid Travel tel: 1-510 285 0640 www.intrepidtravel.com
Dragoman tel: 1-855 273 0866 www.dragoman.co.uk
STA Travel tel: 800-781 4040 www.statravel.com

You can find an even more extensive list of UK providers at the Latin American Travel Association (LATA) Tel: 203 713 6688 www.lata.org

North America
4&5 South America Travel tel: 1-800 747 4540 www.southamerica.travel
Passport: South America www.passportsouthamerica.com (company offering curated trips to Colombia as well as other SA destinations).
Gap Adventures tel: 1-800 553 8701 www.seecolombia.travel

South America
Colombian Highland Tours/Passport: South America tel: 310-552 9079 www.colombianhighlands.com, www.passportsouthamerica.com (joint venture offering tailor-made tours throughout all parts of Colombia, as well as other South American countries).

TRANSPORT

By air. Colombia has a good network of budget domestic airlines that make it cost efficient to fly between cities. No other carrier represents this more than VivaColombia, the country's premier budget airline. In recent years this airline has opened up major routes across Colombia, charging rock-bottom prices for their services. As with many budget airlines, the sheer amount of restrictions and conditions in order to secure a cheap ticket can seem overwhelming. If you don't want to pay hefty extra fees, be prepared to print out their boarding pass and only bring one piece of carry-on luggage.

By sea. In Colombia, water travel is mostly done between countries from Leticia to Brazil and/or Peru. However, a boat trip that is getting increasingly popular is the route from Buenaventura to Bahía Solano, in the Chocó

Department, along Colombia's Pacific coast. Cargo boats leave from the main port every Tuesday night at high tide (leaving for the return trip Saturday at noon), and the journey takes anywhere between 18–24 hours. It costs around US$50 and includes a cramped bunk as well as three meals.

By rail. Like many South American countries, Colombia developed an extensive railroad network around the turn of the 20th century. However, most of these tracks are out of service today. These days most of the rail journeys in Colombia are of the touristic variety. One of the most famous examples is Bogotá's tourist train (www.turistren.com.co), which is a 53km (33-mile) line running from La Sabana station in downtown Bogotá (Calle 13, no. 18-24), stopping in Usaquén and continuing northeast to Zipaquirá, where visitors can visit the famous salt cathedral. Trains run every couple of hours on Saturday and Sunday from 8.15am to 4.40pm and tickets cost around US$17 return.

By bus. The best method for getting around large cities in Colombia is via their metro lines. For example, Bogotá has the Transmilenio (www.transmilenio.gov.co/en), which is the most efficient way of moving quickly around that sprawling metropolis. Rides cost around US$0.75 and are paid for by rechargeable cards, which can be purchased from station tellers (US$1).

For long-distance services from the capital, Bogota's main hub is the **Terminal Central Salitre** (Diagonal 23, no. 69-60; tel: 1-423 3630, extension 145; www.terminaldetransporte.gov.co). Prices for long-distance bus journeys are reasonable, but be prepared to experience an uncomfortable journey. Those traveling the main routes, such as from Bogotá–Cali–Medellín–Cartagena, should find it to be smooth sailing all the way. However, minibuses in the various rural departments and mountain areas have adopted a 'whatever works', approach, and it's not uncommon to find yourself speeding through the hills at breakneck speeds, passing other vehicles on blind curves. That said, at least there's never a dull moment.

By road. Colombia is thankfully blessed with a well-maintained system of highways. Other than in the underfunded Chocó Department where the few in most parts of the country to be in good condition. However, it is wise to be on the lookout for landslides in the wetter and more mountainous areas. They are also relatively easy to navigate across long distances. A couple of roads connect Bogotá with Medellín and the coast, and to the northeast roads run from Boyacá Department to Santander, passing through Bucamaranga and continuing toward Santa Marta, Barranquilla, and Cartagena. Roads also branch off at Bucamaranga and head to Cucuta, at the Venezuelan border. There are also routes from Bogotá over the cordillera to Valle de Cauca and Cali, and all the way down to the border with Ecuador.

> When's the next bus/train to...? **¿Cuándo sale el próximo autobús/tren para...?**
> What's the fare to...? **¿Cuánto es la tarifa a...?**
> A ticket to... **Un billete para...**
> single (one-way) **ida**
> return (roundtrip) **ida y vuelta**

V

VISAS

Colombia typically offers a standard 90-day tourist visa upon arrival. Passports are stamped upon entering the country and you must receive an exit stamp before leaving. If crossing the border overland know that the larger towns and cities often have a Migracion Colombia office, but the smaller ones may not. It's best to get all your requisite passport stamps in the largest city closest to your exit point. Those who are required to apply for a visa before arrival into Colombia include nationals of Bulgaria, Russia, and the Middle East (excluding Israel), Asian countries (excluding Japan, South Korea, Philippines, Indonesia, and Singapore), Haiti, Nicaragua, and all African countries. The visa process is similar from nation to nation: present multiple photos over white background and a completed application form; allow two weeks for processing. If you're in doubt about the visa requirements concerning your home country, check regulations.

You can request a 90-day visa extension, a *salvoconducto*, at any Migracion **Colombia office** (typically only Mon–Fri). The price, as of mid-2018, is around US$33. This will typically be processed on the spot or within 24 hours. Don't apply for the extension any later than 2–3 days before your visa expires. If you do overstay your visa you will incur a fine of around US$133, which only increases the longer you stay

W

WEIGHTS AND MEASURES

Colombia uses the metric system, but uses US gallons for gasoline.

WOMEN TRAVELERS

Solo women travelers should feel safe in Colombia. People are friendly, and if you spend time around families they will likely feel protective of you and take you in as one of their own. As with many countries, foreign women can be the object of unwanted attention from local men, but most Colombian males behave respectively, and catcalls and aggressive flirting are the exception rather than the rule. Still, it's best to always err on the side of caution and never go walking anywhere alone after dark. If you do go out alone, make sure a contact has the details about your location and what time you should return. Feel free to wear a wedding ring, or keep a photograph of a supposed significant other that you can produce when you'd like to rebuff unwanted advances. You can show the photo with a simple *mi marido*, (my husband) or *mi novio* (my boyfriend) and that should diffuse the situation. Knowing at least some Spanish will go a long way to avoiding danger and risky scenarios.

RECOMMENDED HOTELS

The high season for all accommodations is December–February, so plan on paying higher prices during this period. Making reservations through websites like www.booking.com and www.kayak.com is common and efficient.

$$$$	above $150
$$$	$80-150
$$	$30-80
$	$0-30

BOGOTÁ

La Candelaria

Casa Platypus $$ *Carrera 3, no. 12-28;* tel: *1-281 1801;* www.casaplatypusbogota.com. Located in the historic heart of the city, Casa Platypus offers 17 lovely rooms in a well-preserved colonial home. The house is a beautiful throwback complete with balconies with wooden balustrades and a tiled central courtyard with hammocks crisscrossing the beams – perfect for relaxing. There's Wi-fi and cable TV in every room and a continental breakfast of eggs, bread, fruit, fresh juice and coffee. The staff are bilingual and incredibly friendly.

Muisca Hotel $$ *Calle 10, no. 0-25/29;* tel:1-281 0644; www.hotelmuisca.com. This boutique hotel bills itself as "the first pre-Colombian theme hotel" in Bogotá, but the indigenous-inspired interior décor is more tasteful than a gimmick would suggest. In fact, this lodging option is a great find, located in a converted multi-story colonial home with 14 guest rooms. The bar area is cozy, great for imbibing, and the central patio and dining area is a pure colonial dreamscape. Head up the spiral stairs for great views of the neighborhood.

Villa de Leyva

Hostal Renacer $-$$ *Avenida Carrera 10, no. 21 Finca Renacer; tel: 311-308 3739;* www.renacerhostel.com. Owner Oscar has established one of the best lodging options in the city. The location is a former farm one kilometer from the Villa de Leyva's main square that has been converted to a hacienda-like hostel and eco-lodge. It features four and six-bed dorms, plus privates with en-suite bathrooms (the upstairs room boasts the most comfortable mattress in the entire country). There is also camping and sites for motorhomes. The restaurant is open until 9:30pm and the staff are very friendly. The owner also runs the Colombian Highlands tourism agency, meaning you can book excursions from this location.

MEDELLÍN
Centro

Hotel Nutibara $$$$ *Calle 52a, no. 50-46; tel: 4-511 5111;* www.hotelnutibara.com. This was Medellín's first glitzy hotel (opened in 1945), and the elegant rooms today are a bit of a throwback to those days of grandeur. The Art Deco building now includes a sauna and pool as well as all modern amenities. This option is also located next to Plaza Botero.

Poblado

The Black Sheep Hostel $$$ *Transversal 5a, no. 45-133; tel: 4-311 1589;* www.blacksheepmedellin.coma. This is the first-ever hostel in Medellín, and it still enjoys a reputation as one of the best in the city. It's got four, six, eight and 10-bed dorms as well as privates with shared and ensuite bathrooms. They offer free coffee all day and they often do cookouts on the backyard BBQ at weekends.

Pit Stop Guest House $$ *Carrera 43e, no. 51-10; tel: 4-352 1176;* www.pitstopguesthouse.com. Pit Stop has 14 rooms in total, including four doubles with en suite bathrooms; four doubles with shared bathrooms; four group sleeping up to six with en suite bathrooms; and two quadruples with private bathroom. There's a fully equipped games room (Ping Pong, pool table and unmanned bar) with an adjacent steam room and swimming pool in the center of the courtyard. There's a large outdoor meeting area, complete with basketball court in the back. Great meeting spot; relaxed atmosphere.

ANTIOQUIA

Guatapé

Hotel Verony $$$-$$ *Road to El Peñol-Guatapé; tel: 310-833 4101; www.hotelveronyguatape.com.co.* This is a good mid-range option between Guatapé and El Peñol. The rooms are modern and equipped with comfy beds, flat-screen TVs, minibar and showers. Wi-fi works best on the ground floor. Rooms have balconies with great views overlooking the lake. Also has a pool and the restaurant is open until 8pm.

Lake View Hostel $ *Tel: 310-378 8743; www.lakeviewhostel.com.* This good hostel is located on the waterfront in Guatape. There's four, six and eight bed dorms, plus privates with nice views. The hostel arranges tours and activities, like paragliding and motorcycle rental. They even have a Thai restaurant. Breakfast at an additional charge.

Jardín

Hostal Condor de Los Andes $$ *Calle 10, no. 1a-62; tel: 310 379 6069; www.condordelosandeshostal.com.* For the money, this is the best lodging option in town. The Condor has two dorms (five and six-bed bunks) plus 5 privates with en suite bathrooms. The view of the surrounding countryside and river from the leafy patio is worth a million bucks on its own. You can book excursions from here such as to La Cueva del Esplendor, an underwater cave perfect for rappelling. If owner Felipe is in town from Medellín he'll make you feel right at home. You can also book trips to the nearby Adventure Park (complete with human slingshot), from the Condor.

Hotel Jardín $ *Carrera 3, no. 9-14; Hotel Jardín tel: 310-380 6724; www.hoteljardin.com.co.* This colorful hotel in a 100-year-old building was renovated in 2012, and the results speak for themselves. It has retained all its colonial charm, and the central interior courtyard beckons you. Its location on the plaza means it is central, but the adjacent bars can be lively and noisy on weekends.

ZONA CAFETERA

Coffee Fincas and birding retreats

Hacienda Guayabal $$ *Kilometro 3 via Chinchina; tel: 314-772 4856; www.haciendaguayabal.com.* This working coffee finca is located near Chinchina, about 30 minutes away from Manizales. The landscape is impressive: 64 hectares of rolling green coffee fields hugged by bamboo forests. You can stay in the main residence of the family Lodroño, in dorms or privates. Cost includes lodging plus three meals per day. And, naturally, free coffee is included.

Hacienda Venicia $$$ (less for hostel). *3.5 km from Manizales; tel: 320-636 5719; www.haciendavenecia.com.* If you only stay at one coffee finca during your trip to the Zona Cafetera, make sure it is this one. Venecia has been a family-run operation for four generations, and the main hacienda has been in the family since the 1800s. There are three types of accommodation here: the main house, on lush grounds with a pool and elegant rooms filled with family portraits and heirlooms; a guest house; and a recently renovated hostel featuring dorm rooms (great for budget travelers). The English-speaking staff are friendly and the activities on offer include coffee tours and horseback riding.

SANTANDER

San Gil

Hotel Puerto Bahia $$ *Calle 6, no. 9-112; tel: 7-724 4832; www.hotelpuertobahiasangil.com.* This might be the most upscale hotel town. The rooms are decent, and some are decked out with an in-room Jacuzzi. There's a swimming pool and restaurant here. It's very good value for the price.

Macondo Hostel $-$$ *Carrera 8, no. 10-31; tel: 7-724 8001;* www.macondohostel.com. This is the original hostel in San Gil, and it's still the best. The friendly staff has information on every activity in town from adventure sports to free hikes and swimming trips. They can book any excursion. The hostel has three dorm rooms (two four-bed dorms and one 10-bed dorm), six privates (three with en-suite bathrooms), plus a large garden patio with hammocks and Jacuzzi. It's probably the best meeting spot in the city to trade war stories with fellow adrenaline junkies. Be sure to come on *Tejo* night (Tue).

Barichara

Color de Hormiga Hostel $-$$ *Calle 6, no. 5-35; tel: 315- 297 1621;* www.colordehormiga.com. This centrally located hostel (just off the plaza) has seven private rooms (all with ensuite bathrooms), and one nine-bed dorm. There's a great open-air central patio lined with hammocks, greenery and sculptures. There's free coffee in the morning and the friendly staff are ready with maps and info about the town.

CARIBBEAN COAST
Barranquilla

Hotel El Prado $$$ *Carrera 54, no. 70-10; tel: 5-330 1540;* www.hotelelpradobarranquilla.com. This hotel, which has been around since 1930, is the star of Barranquilla. 200 rooms still retain their throwback charm. Also, there are various patios, bars and restaurants ringing a luscious and enormous swimming pool shaded by palms. There's also a gym and tennis courts.

Santa Marta

Aluna Casa y Café $-$$ *Calle 21, no. 5-72; tel: 5-432 4916;* www.alunahotel.com. This central spot has been one of Santa Marta's best budget lodging options for years. It offers the requisite shared dorms, but the privates (all with ensuite bathrooms and some with A/C), situated around a well-lit courtyard, are the best option. There's a kitchen that serves breakfast, lunch and dinner, and the staff are always helpful and friendly.

CARTAGENA

Getsemaní

Media Luna Hostel $ *Calle Media Luna, no. 10-46; tel: 5-664 3423; www.medialunahostel.com.* This is a fun, central hostel with a bar, common area with TV, a cool swimming pool and terrace with views of the neighborhood. The Media Luna offers shared six and eight-bed dorms as well as a triple and private room with fan. They also run Media Luna Playa, on Isla Barú.

Hotel Villa Colonial $$ *Calle de la Medialuna, no. 10; tel: 5-664 4996; www.hotelvillacolonial.com.* The last in the Villa Colonial chain is located on a side street just off the main drag in Getsemaní. Here you'll find peace and quiet and a friendly staff ready to help with tours and rentals. The rooms have A/C and some of them have balconies looking out onto the street.

The walled city

Charleston Santa Teresa $$$$ *Carrera 3, no. 31-23: Centro Plaza de Santa Teresa; tel: 5-664 9494; www.hotelcharlestonsantateresa.com.* This five-star luxury hotel is located in a historic building (a former convent). There are two wings here representing the colonial and republican style of architecture. The rooms are expansive and contain modern and stylish amenities like cable TV and marble bathrooms. There are three restaurants serving fine cuisine, a spa and a tasty pool on the roof with views of the surrounding colonial district.

El Viajero Hostel $-$$ *Calle de los y Infantes, no. 9-45; tel: 318-257 5354.* Part of the Uruguay-based El Viajero chain, the Cartagena location is in a great spot in the San Diego zone. It's a big place with a young vibe, meaning it's basically a party hostel. Still, the staff are friendly and it's well run.

SAN ANDRÉS

Decameron Aquarium $$$$ *Avenida Colombia, no. 1-19; tel: 8-513 0707; www.decameron.com.* Part of the Decameron group of hotels, Aquarium is built over the water on the eastern end of the north peninsula. The hotel's circular design offers panoramic views of the sea, and the rooms (all with terrace or balcony offering sea views) have A/C, minibar, safe and cable TV. There's a dock that leads out to a natural pool where scuba classes are offered. Buffet breakfast is included in the price. Decameron has four other hotels on the island.

La Posada de Lulu $$ *Avenida Antioquia, no. 2-28; tel: 8-512 3416; see Facebook*. This *hospedaje*/hostel option is known as a relaxed no-frills option with attentive service. The space is bright and welcoming and the rooms are clean. It also has two apartments available to rent for longer stays, plus a nice restaurant offering home-cooked food. It's a great mid-range option.

CALI

Central Cali

Hotel Colours $-$$ *Calle 23, no. 2-22; tel: 680 6885; www.colourshotelcali.com*. Colours is a modern budget option. They've managed to strike a nice balance between offering good amenities while keeping prices low. Rooms are bright and colorful and have smart TVs, A/C and minibar. There's a varied breakfast menu as well.

San Antonio and El Peñon

Intercontinental $$$ *Avenida Colombia, no. 2-72; tel: 2-882 3225; www.hotelesestelar.com*. The Intercontinental is part of the Estelar chain of hotels. This 292-room hotel is a pricy option but it's got the amenities to back up the cost. There's a massive pool, sauna, Jacuzzi, travel agency, business center and gym. The rooms are large and have plasma TVs. There are various restaurants here too, as well as a casino.

Posada San Antonio $$ *Carrera 5, no. 3-37; tel: 2-893 7413; www.posadadesanantonio.com*. This hotel is in a beautiful old home with 12 rooms (all with satellite TV, fan and private bathroom) set around a central courtyard and garden. The décor is stylish, with Calima indigenous artifacts throughout. Rates include breakfast and they can arrange salsa classes.

DICTIONARY

ENGLISH-SPANISH

adj adjective **adv** adverb **BE** British English **n** noun **prep** preposition **v** verb

A
abbey la abadía
accept v aceptar
access el acceso
accident el accidente
accommodation el alojamiento
account la cuenta
acupuncture la acupuntura
adapter el adaptador
address la dirección
admission la entrada
after después; **~noon** la tarde; **~shave** el bálsamo para después del afeitado
age la edad
agency la agencia
AIDS el sida
air el aire; **~ conditioning** el aire acondicionado; **~ pump** el aire; **~line** la compañía aérea; **~mail** el correo aéreo; **~plane** el avión; **~port** el aeropuerto
aisle el pasillo; **~ seat** el asiento de pasillo

allergic alérgico; **~ reaction** la reacción alérgica
allow v permitir
alone solo
alter v (clothing) hacer un arreglo
alternate route el otro camino
aluminum foil el papel de aluminio
amazing increíble
ambulance la ambulancia
American estadounidense
amusement park el parque de atracciones
anemic anémico
anesthesia la anestesia
animal el animal
ankle el tobillo
antibiotic el antibiótico
antiques store la tienda de -antigüedades
antiseptic cream la crema antiséptica
anything algo
apartment el apartamento

appendix (body part) el apéndice
appetizer el aperitivo
appointment la cita
arcade el salón de juegos recreativos
area code el prefijo
arm el brazo
aromatherapy la aromaterapia
around (the corner) doblando (la esquina)
arrivals (airport) las llegadas
arrive v llegar
artery la arteria
arthritis la artritis
arts las letras
Asian asiático
aspirin la aspirina
asthmatic asmático
ATM el cajero automático
attack el asalto
attend v asistir
attraction (place) el sitio de interés
attractive guapo
Australia Australia
Australian australiano
automatic automático; **~ car** coche automático
available disponible

B
baby el bebé; **~ bottle** el biberón; **~ wipe** la toallita; **~sitter** el/la canguro
back la espalda; **~ache** el dolor de espalda; **~pack** la mochila
bag la maleta
baggage el equipaje; **~ claim** la recogida de equipajes; **~ ticket** el talón de equipaje
bakery la panadería
ballet el ballet
bandage la tirita
bank el banco
bar el bar
barbecue la barbacoa
barber la peluquería de caballeros
baseball el béisbol
basket (grocery store) la cesta
basketball el baloncesto
bathroom el baño

battery (car) la batería
battery la pila
battleground el campo de batalla
be v ser, estar
beach la playa
beautiful precioso
bed la cama; **~ and breakfast** la pensión
begin v empezar
before antes de
beginner principiante
behind detrás de
beige beis
belt el cinturón
berth la litera
best el/la mejor
better mejor
bicycle la bicicleta
big grande
bigger más grande
bike route el sendero para bicicletas
bikini el biquini; **~ wax** la depilación de las ingles
bill v (charge) cobrar; **~** n (money) el billete; **~** n (of sale) el recibo
bird el pájaro
birthday el cumpleaños
black negro
bladder la vejiga
bland soso
blanket la manta
bleed v sangrar
blood la sangre; **~ pressure** la tensión arterial
blouse la blusa
blue azul

board v embarcar
boarding pass la tarjeta de embarque
boat el barco
bone el hueso
book el libro; **~store** la librería
boots las botas
boring aburrido
botanical garden el jardín botánico
bother v molestar
bottle la botella; **~ opener** el abrebotellas
bowl el cuenco
box la caja
boxing match la pelea de boxeo
boy el niño; **~friend** el novio
bra el sujetador
bracelet la pulsera
brakes (car) los frenos
break v romper
break-in (burglary) el allanamiento de morada
breakdown la avería
breakfast el desayuno
breast el seno; **~feed** dar el pecho
breathe v respirar
bridge el puente
briefs (clothing) los calzoncillos
bring v traer
British británico
broken roto
brooch el broche
broom la escoba
brother el hermano
brown marrón
bug el insecto

building el edificio
burn v (CD) grabar
bus el autobús; **~ station** la estación de autobuses; **~ stop** la parada de autobús; **~ ticket** el billete de autobús; **~ tour** el recorrido en autobús
business los negocios; **~ card** la tarjeta de negocios; **~ center** el centro de negocios; **~ class** la clase preferente; **~ hours** el horario de atención al público
butcher el carnicero
buttocks las nalgas
buy v comprar
bye adiós

C

cabaret el cabaré
cabin (house) la cabaña; **~ (ship)** el camarote
cable car el teleférico
cafe la cafetería
call v llamar; **~** n la llamada
calories las calorías
camera la cámara, **digital ~** la cámara digital; **~ case** la funda para la cámara; **~ store** la tienda de fotografía
camp v acampar; **~ stove** el hornillo; **~site** el cámping

can opener el abrelatas
Canada Canadá
Canadian canadiense
cancel v cancelar
candy el caramelo
canned goods las conservas
canyon el cañón
car el coche; **~ hire [BE]** el alquiler de coches; **~ park [BE]** el aparcamiento; **~ rental** el alquiler de coches; **~ seat** el asiento de niño
carafe la garrafa
card la tarjeta; **ATM ~** la tarjeta de cajero automático; **credit ~** la tarjeta de crédito; **debit ~** la tarjeta de débito; **phone ~** la tarjeta telefónica
carry-on (piece of hand luggage) el equipaje de mano
cart (grocery store) el carrito; **~ (luggage)** el carrito para el equipaje
carton el cartón; **~ of cigarettes** el cartón de tabaco
case (amount) la caja
cash v cobrar; **~** n el efectivo; **~ advance** sacar dinero de la tarjeta
cashier el cajero
casino el casino
castle el castillo
cathedral la catedral

DICTIONARY

cave la cueva
CD el CD
cell phone el teléfono móvil
Celsius el grado centígrado
centimeter el centímetro
certificate el certificado
chair la silla; **~ lift** la telesilla
change v (buses) cambiar; **~** n (money) el cambio
charcoal el carbón
charge v (credit card) cobrar; **~** n (cost) el precio
cheap barato
cheaper más barato
check v (on something) revisar; **~** v (luggage) facturar; **~** n (payment) el cheque; **~-in (airport)** la facturación; **~-in (hotel)** el registro; **~ing account** la cuenta corriente; **~-out (hotel)** la salida
Cheers! ¡Salud!
chemical toilet el váter químico
chemist [BE] la farmacia
cheque [BE] el cheque
chest (body part) el pecho; **~ pain** el dolor de pecho
chewing gum el chicle
child el niño; **~ seat** la silla para niños
children's menu el menú para niños
children's portion la ración para niños
Chinese chino
chopsticks los palillos chinos
church la iglesia
cigar el puro
cigarette el cigarrillo
class la clase; **business ~** la clase preferente; **economy ~** la clase económica; **first ~** la primera clase
classical music la música clásica
clean v limpiar; **~** adj limpio; **~ing product** el producto de limpieza; **~ing supplies** los productos de limpieza
clear v (on an ATM) borrar
cliff el acantilado
cling film [BE] el film transparente
close v (a shop) cerrar
closed cerrado
clothing la ropa; **~ store** la tienda de ropa
club la discoteca
coat el abrigo
coffee shop la cafetería
coin la moneda
colander el escurridor
cold n (sickness) el catarro; **~** adj (temperature) frío
colleague el compañero de trabajo
cologne la colonia
color el color
comb el peine
come v venir
complaint la queja
computer el ordenador
concert el concierto; **~ hall** la sala de conciertos
condition (medical) el estado de salud
conditioner el suavizante
condom el preservativo
conference la conferencia
confirm v confirmar
congestion la congestión
connect v (internet) conectarse
connection (internet) la conexión; **(flight)** la conexión de vuelo
constipated estreñido
consulate el consulado
consultant el consultor
contact v ponerse en contacto con
contact lens la lentilla de contacto; **~ solution** el líquido de lentillas de contacto
contagious contagioso
convention hall el salón de congresos
conveyor belt la cinta transportadora
cook v cocinar
cooking gas el gas butano
cool (temperature) frío
copper el cobre
corkscrew el sacacorchos
cost v costar
cot el catre
cotton el algodón
cough v toser; **~** n la tos
country code el código de país
cover charge la entrada
crash v (car) estrellarse
cream (ointment) la pomada
credit card la tarjeta de crédito
crew neck el cuello redondo
crib la cuna
crystal el cristal
cup la taza
currency la moneda; **~ exchange** el cambio de divisas; **~ exchange office** la casa de cambio
current account [BE] la cuenta corriente
customs las aduanas
cut v (hair) cortar; **~** n (injury) el corte
cute mono
cycling el ciclismo

D

damage v causar daño
damaged ha sufrido daños
dance v bailar; **~ club** la discoteca

dangerous peligroso
dark oscuro
date (calendar) la fecha
day el día
deaf sordo
debit card la tarjeta de débito
deck chair la tumbona
declare v declarar
decline v **(credit card)** rechazar
deeply hondo
degrees (temperature) los grados
delay v retrasarse
delete v **(computer)** borrar
delicatessen la charcutería
delicious delicioso
denim tela vaquero
dentist el dentista
denture la dentadura
deodorant el desodorante
department store los grandes almacenes
departures (airport) las salidas
deposit v depositar; ~ n **(bank)** el depósito bancario; ~ v **(reserve a room)** la fianza
desert el desierto
dessert el postre
detergent el detergente
develop v **(film)** revelar
diabetic diabético
dial v marcar
diamond el diamante

diaper el pañal
diarrhea la diarrea
diesel el diesel
difficult difícil
digital digital; ~ **camera** la cámara digital; ~ **photos** las fotos digitales; ~ **prints** las fotos digitales
dining room el comedor
dinner la cena
direction la dirección
dirty sucio
disabled discapacitado; ~ **accessible [BE]** el acceso para discapacitados
discharge (bodily fluid) la secreción
disconnect (computer) desconectar
discount el descuento
dish (kitchen) el plato; ~**washer** el lavavajillas; ~**washing liquid** el líquido lavavajillas
display v mostrar; ~ **case** la vitrina
disposable desechable; ~ **razor** la cuchilla desechable
dive v bucear
diving equipment el equipo de buceo
divorce v divorciar
dizzy mareado
doctor el médico
doll la muñeca
dollar (U.S.) el dólar
domestic nacional;

~ **flight** el vuelo nacional
door la puerta
dormitory el dormitorio
double bed la cama de matrimonio
downtown el centro
dozen la docena
drag lift el telesquí
dress (piece of clothing) el vestido; ~ **code** las normas de vestuario
drink v beber; ~ n la bebida; ~ **menu** la carta de bebidas; ~**ing water** el agua potable
drive v conducir
driver's license number el número de permiso de conducir
drop (medicine) la gota
drowsiness la somnolencia
dry cleaner la tintorería
dubbed doblada
during durante
duty (tax) el impuesto; ~-**free** libre de impuestos
DVD el DVD

E

ear la oreja; ~**ache** el dolor de oído
earlier más temprano
early temprano
earrings los pendientes

east el este
easy fácil
eat v comer
economy class la clase económica
elbow el codo
electric outlet el enchufe eléctrico
elevator el ascensor
e-mail v enviar un correo electrónico; ~ n el correo electrónico; ~ **address** la dirección de correo electrónico
emergency la emergencia; ~ **exit** la salida de urgencia
empty v vaciar
enamel (jewelry) el esmalte
end v terminar
English el inglés
engrave v grabar
enjoy v disfrutar
enter v entrar
entertainment el entretenimiento
entrance la entrada
envelope el sobre
equipment el equipo
escalators las escaleras mecánicas
e-ticket el billete electrónico
EU resident el/la residente de la UE
euro el euro
evening la noche
excess el exceso
exchange (money) cambiar; ~ v **(goods)** devolver; ~ n **(place)** la casa

de cambio; **~ rate** el tipo de cambio
excursion la excursión
excuse v **(to get past)** pedir perdón; **~** v **(to get attention)** disculparse
exhausted agotado
exit v salir; **~** n la salida
expensive caro
expert (skill level) experto
exposure (film) la foto
express rápido; **~ bus** el autobús rápido; **~ train** el tren rápido
extension (phone) la extensión
extra adicional; **~ large** equis ele (XL)
extract v **(tooth)** extraer
eye el ojo
eyebrow wax la depilación de cejas

F

face la cara
facial la limpieza de cutis
family la familia
fan (appliance) el ventilador; **~ (souvenir)** el abanico
far lejos; **~-sighted** hipermétrope
farm la granja
fast rápido; **~ food** la comida rápida
faster más rápido
fat free sin grasa
father el padre

fax v enviar un fax; **~** n el fax; **~ number** el número de fax
fee la tasa
feed v alimentar
ferry el ferry
fever la fiebre
field (sports) el campo
fill v llenar ; **~ out (form)** rellenar
filling (tooth) el empaste
film (camera) el carrete
fine (fee for breaking law) la multa
finger el dedo; **~nail** la uña del dedo
fire fuego; **~ department** los bomberos; **~ door** la puerta de incendios
first primero; **~ class** la primera clase
fit (clothing) quedar bien
fitting room el probador
fix v **(repair)** reparar
flashlight la linterna
flight el vuelo
floor el suelo
flower la flor
folk music la música folk
food la comida
foot el pie
football [BE] el fútbol
for para/por
forecast el pronóstico

forest el bosque
fork el tenedor
form el formulario
formula (baby) la fórmula infantil
fort el fuerte
fountain la fuente
free gratuito
freezer el congelador
fresh fresco
friend el amigo
frying pan la sartén
full completo; **~-service** el servicio completo; **~-time** a tiempo completo

G

game el partido
garage (parking) el garaje; **~ (repair)** el taller
garbage bag la bolsa de basura
gas la gasolina; **~ station** la gasolinera
gate (airport) la puerta
gay gay; **~ bar** el bar gay; **~ club** la discoteca gay
gel (hair) la gomina
get to v ir a
get off v **(a train/bus/subway)** bajarse
gift el regalo; **~ shop** la tienda de regalos
girl la niña; **~friend** la novia
give v dar
glass (drinking) el vaso; **~ (material)** el vidrio

glasses las gafas
go v **(somewhere)** ir a
gold el oro
golf golf; **~ course** el campo de golf; **~ tournament** el torneo de golf
good n el producto; **~** adj bueno; **~ afternoon** buenas tardes; **~ evening** buenas noches; **~ morning** buenos días; **~bye** adiós
gram el gramo
grandchild el nieto
grandparent el abuelo
gray gris
green verde
grocery store el supermercado
ground la tierra; **~ floor** la planta baja; **~cloth** la tela impermeable
group el grupo
guide el guía; **~ book** la guía; **~ dog** el perro guía
gym el gimnasio
gynecologist el ginecólogo

H

hair el pelo; **~ dryer** el secador de pelo; **~ salon** la peluquería; **~brush** el cepillo de pelo; **~cut** el corte de pelo; **~spray** la laca; **~style** el peinado; **~stylist** el

estilista
half medio; **~ hour** la media hora; **~-kilo** el medio kilo
hammer el martillo
hand la mano; **~ luggage [BE]** el equipaje de mano; **~bag [BE]** el bolso
handicapped discapacitado; **~-accessible** el acceso para discapacitados
hangover la resaca
happy feliz
hat el sombrero
have *v* tener
head (body part) la cabeza; **~ache** el dolor de cabeza; **~phones** los cascos
health la salud; **~ food store** la tienda de alimentos naturales
heart el corazón; **~ condition** padecer del corazón
heat *v* calentar; **~** *n* el calor
heater [heating BE] la calefacción
hello hola
helmet el casco
help *v* ayudar; **~** *n* la ayuda
here aquí
hi hola
high alto; **~chair** la trona; **~way** la autopista
hiking boots las botas de montaña
hill la colina

hire *v* **[BE]** alquilar; **~ car [BE]** el coche de alquiler
hitchhike *v* hacer autostop
hockey el hockey
holiday [BE] las vacaciones
horse track el hipódromo
hospital el hospital
hostel el albergue
hot (temperature) caliente; **~ (spicy)** picante; **~ spring** el agua termale; **~ water** el agua caliente
hotel el hotel
hour la hora
house la casa; **~hold goods** los artículos para el hogar; **~keeping services** el servicio de limpieza de habitaciones
how (question) cómo; **~ much (question)** cuánto cuesta
hug *v* abrazar
hungry hambriento
hurt *v* **(have pain)** tener dolor
husband el marido

I

ibuprofen el ibuprofeno
ice el hielo; **~ hockey** el hockey sobre hielo
icy *adj* helado
identification el docu-

mento de identidad
ill *v* **(to feel)** encontrarse mal
in dentro
include *v* incluir
indoor pool la piscina cubierta
inexpensive barato
infected infectado
information (phone) el número de teléfono de información; **~ desk** el mostrador de información
insect el insecto; **~ bite** la picadura de insecto; **~ repellent** el repelente de insectos
insert *v* introducir
insomnia el insomnio
instant message el mensaje instantáneo
insulin la insulina
insurance el seguro; **~ card** la tarjeta de seguro; **~ company** la compañía de seguros
interesting interesante
intermediate el nivel intermedio
international (airport area) internacional; **~ flight** el vuelo internacional; **~ student card** la tarjeta internacional de estudiante
internet la internet; **~ cafe** el cibercafé; **~ service** el servicio de internet; **wire-**

less **~** el acceso inalámbrico
interpreter el/la intérprete
intersection el cruce
intestine el intestino
introduce *v* presentar
invoice [BE] la factura
Ireland Irlanda
Irish irlandés
iron *v* planchar; **~** *n* **(clothes)** la plancha
Italian italiano

J

jacket la chaqueta
jar el bote
jaw la mandíbula
jazz el jazz; **~ club** el club de jazz
jeans los vaqueros
jet ski la moto acuática
jeweler la joyería
jewelry las joyas
join *v* acompañar a
joint (body part) la articulación

K

key la llave; **~ card** la llave electrónica; **~ ring** el llavero
kiddie pool la piscina infantil
kidney (body part) el riñón
kilo el kilo; **~gram** el kilogramo; **~meter** el kilómetro
kiss *v* besar
kitchen la cocina; **~ foil [BE]** el papel de aluminio

knee la rodilla
knife el cuchillo

L

lace el encaje
lactose intolerant alérgico a la lactosa
lake el lago
large grande; **~er** más grande
last último
late (time) tarde; **~er** más tarde
launderette [BE] la lavandería
laundromat la lavandería
laundry la colada; **~ facility** la lavandería; **~ service** el servicio de lavandería
lawyer el abogado
leather el cuero
to leave v salir
left (direction) la izquierda
leg la pierna
lens la lente
less menos
lesson la lección
letter la carta
library la biblioteca
life la vida; **~ jacket** el chaleco salvavidas; **~guard** el socorrista
lift n [BE] el ascensor; **~ (to give a ride)** llevar en coche; **~ pass** el pase de acceso a los remontes
light n **(overhead)** la luz; v **~ (ciga-**
rette) dar fuego; **~bulb** la bombilla
lighter el mechero
like v gustar; **I like me gusta**
line (train) la línea
linen el lino
lip el labio
liquor store la tienda de bebidas alcohólicas
liter el litro
little pequeño
live v vivir
liver (body part) el hígado
loafers los mocasines
local de la zona
lock v cerrar; **~** n el cerrojo
locker la taquilla
log on v **(computer)** iniciar sesión
log off v **(computer)** cerrar sesión
long largo; **~ sleeves** las mangas largas; **~-sighted [BE]** hipermétrope
look v mirar
lose v **(something)** perder
lost perdido; **~ and found** la oficina de objetos perdidos
lotion la crema hidratante
louder más alto
love v querer; **~** n el amor
low bajo; **~er** más bajo
luggage el equipaje; **~ cart** el carrito de

equipaje; **~ locker** la consigna automática; **~ ticket** el talón de equipaje; **hand ~ [BE]** el equipaje de mano
lunch la comida
lung el pulmón

M

magazine la revista
magnificent magnifico
mail v enviar por correo; **~** n el correo; **~box** el buzón de correo
main principal; **~ attractions** los principales sitios de interés; **~ course** el plato principal
make up a prescription v **[BE]** despachar medicamentos
mall el centro comercial
man el hombre
manager el gerente
manicure la manicura
manual car el coche con transmisión manual
map el mapa
market el mercado
married casado
marry v casarse
mass (church service) la misa
massage el masaje
match la cerilla
meal la comida
measure v **(some-**

one) medir
measuring cup la taza medidora
measuring spoon la cuchara medidora
mechanic el mecánico
medicine el medicamento
medium (size) mediano
meet v **(someone)** conocer
meeting la reunión; **~ room** la sala de reuniones
membership card la tarjeta de socio
memorial (place) el monumento conmemorativo
memory card la tarjeta de memoria
mend v zurcir
menstrual cramps los dolores menstruales
menu la carta
message el mensaje
meter (parking) el parquímetro
microwave el microondas
midday [BE] el mediodía
midnight la medianoche
mileage el kilometraje
mini-bar el minibar
minute el minuto
missing desaparecido
mistake el error
mobile móvil; **~ home** la caravana; **~ phone [BE]**

el teléfono móvil
mobility la movilidad
money el dinero
month el mes
mop la fregona
moped el ciclomotor
more más
morning la mañana
mosque la mezquita
mother la madre
motion sickness el mareo
motor el motor; **~boat** la lancha motora; **~cycle** la motocicleta; **~way [BE]** la autopista
mountain la montaña; **~bike** la bicicleta de montaña
mousse (hair) la espuma para el pelo
mouth *n* la boca
movie la película; **~theater** el cine
mug *v* asaltar
muscle (body part) el músculo
museum el museo
music la música; **~store** la tienda de música

N

nail la u͞na; **~file** la lima de uñas; **~salon** el salon de manicura
name el nombre
napkin la servilleta
nappy [BE] el pañale
nationality la nacionalidad
nature preserve la reserva natural
(be) nauseous *v* tener náuseas
near cerca; **~-sighted** miope; **~by** cerca de aquí
neck el cuello
necklace el collar
need *v* necesitar
newspaper el periódico
newsstand el quiosco
next próximo
nice *adj* amable
night la noche; **~club** la discoteca
no no
non sin; **~-alcoholic** sin alcohol; **~-smoking** para no fumadores
noon el mediodía
north el norte
nose la nariz
note [BE] el billete
nothing nada
notify *v* avisar
novice (skill level) principiante
now ahora
number el número
nurse el enfermero/la enfermera

O

office la oficina; **~hours (doctor's)** las horas de consulta; **~hours (other offices)** el horario de oficina
off-licence [BE] la tienda de bebidas alcohólicas
oil el aceite
OK de acuerdo
old *adj* viejo
on the corner en la esquina
once una vez
one uno; **~-way ticket** el billete de ida; **~-way street** la calle de sentido único
only solamente
open *v* abrir; **~** *adj* abierto
opera la ópera; **~house** el teatro de la ópera
opposite frente a
optician el oculista
orange (color) naranja
orchestra la orquesta
order *v* pedir
outdoor pool la piscina exterior
outside fuera
over sobre; **~the counter (medication)** sin receta; **~look (scenic place)** el mirador; **~night** por la noche
oxygen treatment la oxigenoterapia

P

p.m. de la tarde
pacifier el chupete
pack *v* hacer las maletas
package el paquete
paddling pool [BE] la piscina infantil
pad [BE] la compresa
pain el dolor
pajamas los pijamas
palace el palacio
pants los pantalones
pantyhose las medias
paper el papel; **~towel** el papel de cocina
paracetamol [BE] el paracetamol
park *v* aparcar; **~** *n* el parque; **~ing garage** el párking; **~ing lot** el aparcamiento
parliament building el palacio de las cortes
part (for car) la pieza; **~-time** a tiempo parcial
pass through *v* estar de paso
passenger el pasajero
passport el pasaporte; **~control** el control de pasaportes
password la contraseña
pastry shop la pastelería
path el camino
pay *v* pagar; **~phone** el teléfono público
peak (of a mountain) la cima
pearl la perla
pedestrian el peatón
pediatrician el pediatra
pedicure la pedicura
pen el bolígrafo

DICTIONARY 149

penicillin la penicilina
penis el pene
per por; **~ day** por día; **~ hour** por hora; **~ night** por noche; **~ week** por semana
perfume el perfume
period (menstrual) la regla; **~ (of time)** la época
permit v permitir
petite las tallas pequeñas
petrol la gasolina; **~ station** la gasolinera
pewter el peltre
pharmacy la farmacia
phone v hacer una llamada; **~** n el teléfono; **~ call** la llamada de teléfono; **~ card** la tarjeta telefónica; **~ number** el número de teléfono
photo la foto; **~copy** la fotocopia; **~graphy** la fotografía
pick up v (something) recoger
picnic area la zona para picnic
piece el trozo
Pill (birth control) la píldora
pillow la almohada
personal identification number (PIN) la clave
pink rosa

piste [BE] la pista; **~ map [BE]** el mapa de pistas
pizzeria la pizzería
place v (a bet) hacer una apuesta
plane el avión
plastic wrap el film transparente
plate el plato
platform [BE] (train) el andén
platinum el platino
play v jugar; **~** n (theater) la obra de teatro; **~ground** el patio de recreo; **~pen** el parque
please por favor
pleasure el placer
plunger el desatascador
plus size la talla grande
pocket el bolsillo
poison el veneno
poles (skiing) los bastones
police la policía; **~ report** el certificado de la policía; **~ station** la comisaría
pond el estanque
pool la piscina
pop music la música pop
portion la ración
post [BE] el correo; **~ office** la oficina de correos; **~box [BE]** el buzón de correos; **~card** la tarjeta postal
pot la olla

pottery la cerámica
pounds (British sterling) las libras esterlinas
pregnant embarazada
prescribe v recetar
prescription la receta
press v (clothing) planchar
price el precio
print v imprimir
problem el problema
produce las frutas o verduras; **~ store** la frutería y verdulería
prohibit v prohibir
pronounce v pronunciar
public el público
pull v (door sign) tirar
purple morado
purse el bolso
push v (door sign) empujar; **~chair [BE]** el cochecito de niño

Q

quality n la calidad
question la pregunta
quiet adj tranquilo

R

racetrack el circuito de carreras
racket (sports) la raqueta
railway station [BE] la estación de trenes
rain la lluvia; **~coat** el chubasquero; **~forest** el bosque pluvial;

~y adv lluvioso
rap (music) el rap
rape v violar; **~** n la violación
rash la erupción cutánea
razor blade la hoja de afeitar
reach v localizar
ready listo
real auténtico
receipt el recibo
receive v recibir
reception la recepción
recharge v recargar
recommend v recomendar
recommendation la recomendación
recycle v reciclar
red rojo
refrigerator n la nevera
region la región
registered mail el correo certificado
regular normal
relationship la relación
rent v alquilar
rental car el coche de alquiler
repair v arreglar
repeat v repetir
reservation la reserva; **~ desk** la taquilla
reserve v reservar
restaurant el restaurante
restroom el servicio
retired jubilado
return v (something) devolver; **~** n [BE] la ida y vuelta

rib (body part) la costilla
right (direction) derecha; **~ of way** prioridad de paso
ring el anillo
river n el río
road map el mapa de carreteras
rob v atracar
robbed atracado
romantic romántico
room la habitación; **~ key** la llave de habitación; **~ service** el servicio de habitaciones
round-trip ida y vuelta
route la ruta
rowboat la barca de remos
rubbish [BE] la basura; **~ bag [BE]** la bolsa de basura
rugby el rugby
ruins las ruinas
rush la prisa

S

sad triste
safe n la caja fuerte; **~** adj seguro
sales tax el IVA
same mismo
sandals las sandalias
sanitary napkin la compresa
saucepan el cazo
sauna la sauna
save v (computer) guardar
savings (account) la cuenta de ahorro
scanner el escáner

scarf la bufanda
schedule v programar; **~** n el horario
school el colegio
science la ciencia
scissors las tijeras
sea el mar
seat el asiento
security la seguridad
see v ver
self-service el autoservicio
sell v vender
seminar el seminario
send v enviar
senior citizen jubilado
separated (marriage) -separado
serious serio
service (in a restaurant) el servicio
sexually transmitted disease (STD) la enfermedad de transmisión sexual
shampoo el champú
sharp afilado
shaving cream la crema de afeitar
sheet la sábana
ship v enviar
shirt la camisa
shoe store la zapatería
shoes los zapatos
shop v comprar
shopping ir de compras; **~ area** la zona de compras; **~ centre [BE]** el centro comercial; **~ mall** el centro comercial
short corto; **~ sleeves** las mangas cortas;

~s los pantalones cortos; **~-sighted [BE]** miope
shoulder el hombro
show v enseñar
shower la ducha
shrine el santuario
sick enfermo
side el lado; **~ dish** la guarnición; **~ effect** el efecto secundario; **~ order** la guarnición
sightsee v hacer turismo
sightseeing tour el recorrido turístico
sign v (name) firmar
silk la seda
silver la plata
single (unmarried) soltero; **~ bed** la cama; **~ prints** una copia; **~ room** una habitación individual
sink el lavabo
sister la hermana
sit v sentarse
size la talla
skin la piel
skirt la falda
ski v esquiar; **~** n el esquí; **~ lift** el telesquí
sleep v dormir; **~er car** el coche cama; **~ing bag** el saco de dormir
slice v cortar en rodajas
slippers las zapatillas
slower más despacio
slowly despacio

small pequeño
smaller más pequeño
smoke v fumar
smoking (area) la zona de fumadores
snack bar la cafetería
sneakers las zapatillas de deporte
snorkeling equipment el equipo de esnórquel
snow la nieve; **~board** la tabla de snowboard; **~shoe** la raqueta de nieve; **~y** nevado
soap el jabón
soccer el fútbol
sock el calcetín
some alguno
soother [BE] el chupete
sore throat las anginas
sorry lo siento
south el sur
souvenir el recuerdo; **~ store** la tienda de recuerdos
spa el centro de salud y belleza
Spain España
Spanish el español
spatula la espátula
speak v hablar
special (food) la especialidad de la casa
specialist (doctor) el especialista
specimen el ejemplar
speeding el exceso de velocidad
spell v deletrear

DICTIONARY

spicy picante
spine (body part) la columna vertebral
spoon la cuchara
sports los deportes; **~ massage** el masaje deportivo
sporting goods store la tienda de deportes
sprain el esguince
square cuadrado; **~ kilometer** el kilómetro cuadrado; **~ meter** el metro cuadrado
stadium el estadio
stairs las escaleras
stamp v **(a ticket)** picar; **~** n **(postage)** el sello
start v empezar
starter [BE] el aperitivo
station la estación; **bus ~** la estación de autobuses; **gas ~** la gasolinera; **muster ~ [BE]** el punto de reunión; **petrol ~ [BE]** la gasolinera; **subway ~** el metro; **train ~** la estación de tren
statue la estatua
stay v quedarse
steal v robar
steep empinado
sterling silver la plata esterlina
sting el escozor
stolen robado
stomach el estómago;

~ache el dolor de estómago
stop v pararse; **~** n la parada
storey [BE] la planta
stove el horno
straight recto
strange extraño
stream el arroyo
stroller el cochecito
student el estudiante
study v estudiar
stunning impresionante
subtitle el subtítulo
subway el metro; **~ station** la estación de metro
suit el traje
suitcase la maleta
sun el sol; **~block** el protector solar total; **~burn** la quemadura solar; **~glasses** las gafas de sol; **~ny** soleado; **~screen** el protector solar; **~stroke** la insolación
super (fuel) súper; **~market** el supermercado
surfboard la tabla de surf
surgical spirit [BE] el alcohol etílico
swallow v tragar
sweater el jersey
sweatshirt la sudadera
sweet (taste) dulce; **~s [BE]** los caramelos
swelling la hinchazón

swim v nadar; **~suit** el bañador
symbol (keyboard) el símbolo
synagogue la sinagoga

T

table la mesa
tablet (medicine) el comprimido
take v llevar; **~ away [BE]** para llevar
tampon el tampón
tapas bar el bar de tapas
taste v probar
taxi el taxi
team el equipo
telephone el teléfono
temporary provisional
tennis el tenis
tent la tienda de campaña; **~ peg** la estaca; **~ pole** el mástil
terminal (airport) la terminal
terracotta la terracotta
terrible terrible
text v **(send a message)** enviar un mensaje de texto; **~** n **(message)** el texto
thank v dar las gracias a; **~ you** gracias
that eso
theater el teatro
there ahí
thief el ladrón
thigh el muslo
thirsty sediento

this esto
throat la garganta
ticket el billete; **~ office** el despacho de billetes; **~ed passenger** el pasajero con billete
tie (clothing) la corbata
time el tiempo; **~table [BE]** el horario
tire la rueda
tired cansado
tissue el pañuelo de papel
tobacconist el estanco
today hoy
toe el dedo del pie; **~nail** la uña del pie
toilet [BE] el servicio; **~ paper** el papel higiénico
tomorrow mañana
tongue la lengua
tonight esta noche
too demasiado
tooth el diente; **~brush** el cepillo de dientes; **~paste** la pasta de dientes
total (amount) el total
tough (food) duro
tourist el turista; **~ information office** la oficina de turismo
tour el recorrido turístico
tow truck la grúa
towel la toalla
tower la torre
town la ciudad; **~ hall** el ayuntamiento; **~**

151

map el mapa de ciudad; **~ square** la plaza
toy el juguete; **~ store** la tienda de juguetes
track (train) el andén
traditional tradicional
traffic light el semáforo
trail la pista; **~ map** el mapa de la pista
trailer el remolque
train el tren; **~ station** la estación de tren
transfer *v* cambiar
translate *v* traducir
trash la basura
travel *v* viajar; **~ agency** la agencia de viajes; **~ sickness** el mareo; **~er's check [cheque BE]** el cheque de viaje
tree el árbol
trim (hair cut) cortarse las puntas
trip el viaje
trolley [BE] el carrito
trousers [BE] los pantalones
T-shirt la camiseta
turn off *v* apagar
turn on *v* encender
TV la televisión
type *v* escribir a máquina
tyre [BE] la rueda

U

United Kingdom (U.K.) el Reino Unido
United States (U.S.) los Estados Unidos
ugly feo
umbrella el paraguas
unattended desatendido
unconscious inconsciente
underground [BE] el metro; **~ station [BE]** la estación de metro
underpants [BE] los calzoncillos
understand *v* entender
underwear la ropa interior
university la universidad
unleaded (gas) la gasolina sin plomo
upper superior
urgent urgente
use *v* usar
username el nombre de usuario
utensil el cubierto

V

vacancy la habitación libre
vacation las vacaciones
vaccination la vacuna
vacuum cleaner la aspiradora
vaginal infection la infección vaginal
valid validez
valley el valle
valuable valioso
VAT [BE] el IVA
vegetarian vegetariano
vehicle registration el registro del coche
viewpoint [BE] el mirador
village el pueblo
vineyard la viña
visa (passport document) el visado
visit *v* visitar; **~ing hours** el horario de visita
visually impaired la persona con discapacidad visual
vitamin la vitamina
V-neck el cuello de pico
vomit *v* vomitar

W

wait *v* esperar; **~** *n* la espera; **~ing room** la sala de espera
waiter el camarero
waitress la camarera
wake *v* despertarse; **~-up call** la llamada despertador
walk *v* caminar; **~** *n* la caminata; **~ing route** la ruta de senderismo
wallet la cartera
warm *v* **(something)** calentar; **~** *adj* **(temperature)** calor
washing machine la lavadora
watch el reloj
waterfall la cascada
weather el tiempo
week la semana; **~end** el fin de semana; **~ly** semanal
welcome *v* acoger
well bien; **~-rested** descansado
west el oeste
what (question) qué
wheelchair la silla de ruedas; **~ ramp** la rampa para silla de ruedas
when (question) cuándo
where (question) dónde
white blanco; **~ gold** el oro blanco
who (question) quién
widowed viudo
wife la mujer
window la ventana; **~ case** el escaparate
windsurfer el surfista
wine list la carta de vinos
wireless inalámbrico; **~ internet** el acceso inalámbrico a internet; **~ internet service** el servicio inalámbrico a internet; **~ phone** el teléfono móvil
with con
withdraw *v* retirar; **~al (bank)** retirar fondos
without sin
woman la mujer
wool la lana

DICTIONARY

work v trabajar
wrap v envolver
wrist la muñeca
write v escribir

Y

year el año
yellow amarillo
yes sí

yesterday ayer
young joven
youth hostel el albergue juvenil

Z

zoo el zoológico

SPANISH-ENGLISH

A

a tiempo completo full-time
a tiempo parcial part-time
la abadía abbey
el abanico fan (souvenir)
abierto adj open
el abogado lawyer
abrazar v hug
el abrebotellas bottle opener
el abrelatas can opener
el abrigo coat
abrir v open
el abuelo grandparent
aburrido boring
acampar v camp
el acantilado cliff
el acceso access; **~ inalámbrico a internet** wireless internet; **~ para discapacitados** handicapped- [disabled- BE] accessible
el accidente accident
el aceite oil
aceptar v accept
acoger v welcome
acompañar a v join
la acupuntura acupuncture
el adaptador adapter
adicional extra
adiós goodbye
las aduanas customs
el aeropuerto airport
afilado sharp
la agencia agency; **~ de viajes** travel agency
agotado exhausted
el agua water; **~ caliente** hot water; **~ potable** drinking water
las aguas termales hot spring
ahí there
ahora now
el aire air, air pump; **~ acondicionado** air conditioning
el albergue hostel; **~ juvenil** youth hostel
alérgico allergic; **~ a la lactosa** lactose intolerant
algo anything
el algodón cotton
alguno some
alimentar v feed
el allanamiento de morada break-in (burglary)
la almohada pillow
el alojamiento accommodation
alquilar v rent [hire BE]; **el ~ de coches** car rental [hire BE]
alto high
amable nice
amarillo yellow
la ambulancia ambulance
el amigo friend
el amor n love
el andén track [platform BE] (train)
anémico anemic
la anestesia anesthesia
las anginas sore throat
el anillo ring
el animal animal
antes de before
el antibiótico antibiotic
el año year
apagar v turn off
el aparcamiento parking lot [car park BE]
aparcar v park
el apartamento apartment
el apéndice appendix (body part)
el aperitivo appetizer [starter BE]
aquí here
el árbol tree
la aromaterapia aromatherapy
arreglar v repair
el arroyo stream
la arteria artery
la articulación joint (body part)
los artículos goods; **~ para el hogar** household good
la artritis arthritis
asaltar v mug
el asalto attack
el ascensor elevator [lift BE]
asiático Asian
el asiento seat; **~ de niño** car seat; **~ de pasillo** aisle seat
asistir v attend
asmático asthmatic
la aspiradora vacuum cleaner
la aspirina aspirin
atracado robbed
atracar v rob
Australia Australia

australiano Australian
auténtico real
el autobús bus; **~ rápido** express bus
automático automatic
la autopista highway [motorway BE]
el autoservicio self-service
la avería breakdown
el avión airplane, plane
avisar v notify
ayer yesterday
la ayuda n help
ayudar v help
el ayuntamiento town hall
azul blue

B

bailar v dance
bajarse v get off (a train, bus, subway)
bajo low
el ballet ballet
el baloncesto basketball
el bálsamo para después del afeitado aftershave
el banco bank
el bañador swimsuit
el baño bathroom
el bar bar; **~ de tapas** tapas bar; **~ gay** gay bar
barato cheap, inexpensive
la barbacoa barbecue
la barca de remos rowboat
el barco boat
los bastones poles (skiing)
la basura trash [rubbish BE]
la batería battery (car)
el bebé baby
beber v drink
la bebida n drink
beis beige
el béisbol baseball
besar v kiss
el biberón baby bottle
la biblioteca library
la bicicleta bicycle; **~ de montaña** mountain bike
el billete n bill (money); **~** ticket; **~ de autobús** bus ticket; **~ de ida** one-way (ticket); **~ de ida y vuelta** round trip [return BE]; **~ electrónico** e-ticket
el biquini bikini
blanco white
la blusa blouse
la boca mouth
el bolígrafo pen
la bolsa de basura garbage [rubbish BE] bag
el bolsillo pocket
el bolso purse [handbag BE]
los bomberos fire department
la bombilla lightbulb
borrar v clear (on an ATM); **~** v delete (computer)
el bosque forest; **~ pluvial** rainforest
las botas boots; **~ de montaña** hiking boots
el bote jar
la botella bottle
el brazo arm
británico British
el broche brooch
bucear to dive
bueno adj good
buenas noches good evening
buenas tardes good afternoon
buenos días good morning
la bufanda scarf
el buzón de correo mailbox [postbox BE]

C

la cabaña cabin (house)
el cabaré cabaret
la cabeza head (body part)
la cafetería cafe, coffee shop, snack bar
la caja case (amount); **~ fuerte** n safe
el cajero cashier; **~ automático** ATM
el calcetín sock
la calefacción heater [heating BE]
calentar v heat, warm
la calidad quality
la calle de sentido único one-way street
calor hot, warm (temperature)
las calorías calories
los calzoncillos briefs [underpants BE] (clothing)
la cama single bed; **~ de matrimonio** double bed
la cámara camera; **~ digital** digital camera
la camarera waitress
el camarero waiter
el camarote cabin (ship)
cambiar v change, exchange, transfer
el cambio n change (money); **~ de divisas** currency exchange
caminar v walk
la caminata n walk
el camino path
la camisa shirt
la camiseta T-shirt
el cámping campsite
el campo field (sports); **~ de batalla** battleground; **~ de golf** golf course
Canadá Canada
canadiense Canadian
cancelar v cancel
el/la canguro babysitter
cansado tired
el cañón canyon
la cara face
los caramelos candy [sweets BE]
la caravana mobile home
el carbón charcoal
el carnicero butcher
caro expensive

el carrete film (camera)
el carrito cart [trolley BE] (grocery store); **~ de equipaje** luggage cart
la carta letter
la carta n menu; **~ de bebidas** drink menu; **~ para niños** children's menu; **~ de vinos** wine list
la cartera n wallet
el cartón carton; **~ de tabaco** carton of cigarettes
la casa house; **~ de cambio** currency exchange office
casado married
casarse v marry
la cascada waterfall
el casco helmet
los cascos headphones
el casino casino
el castillo castle
el catarro cold (sickness)
la catedral cathedral
el catre cot
causar daño v damage
el cazo saucepan
el CD CD
la cena dinner
el centímetro centimeter
el centro downtown area; **~ comercial** shopping mall [centre BE]; **~ de negocios** business center; **~ de salud y belleza** spa
el cepillo de pelo hair brush
la cerámica pottery
cerca near; **~ de aquí** nearby
la cerilla n match
cerrado closed
cerrar v close, lock; **~ sesión** v log off (computer)
el cerrojo n lock
el certificado certificate; **~ de la policía** police report
la cesta basket (grocery store)
el chaleco salvavidas life jacket
el champú shampoo
la chaqueta jacket
la charcutería delicatessen
el cheque n check [cheque BE] (payment); **~ de viaje** traveler's check [cheque BE]
el chicle chewing gum
chino Chinese
el chubasquero raincoat
el chupete pacifier [soother BE]
el cibercafé internet cafe
el ciclismo cycling
el ciclomotor moped
la ciencia science
el cigarrillo cigarette
la cima peak (of a mountain)
el cine movie theater
la cinta transportadora conveyor belt
el cinturón n belt
el circuito de carreras racetrack
la cita appointment
la ciudad town
la clase class; **~ económica** economy class; **preferente** business class
la clave personal identification number (PIN)
el club de jazz jazz club
cobrar v bill (charge); **~** v cash; **~** v charge (credit card)
el cobre copper
el coche n car; **~ de alquiler** rental [hire BE] car; **~ automático** automatic car; **~ cama** sleeper [sleeping BE] car; **~ con transmisión manual** manual car
el cochecito stroller [pushchair BE]
la cocina kitchen
cocinar v cook
el código de país country code
el codo elbow
la colada laundry
el colegio school
la colina hill
el collar necklace
la colonia cologne
el color color
la columna vertebral spine (body part)
el comedor dining room
comer v eat
la comida food, lunch, meal; **~ rápida** fast food
la comisaría police station
cómo how
el compañero de trabajo colleague
la compañía company; **~ aérea** airline; **~ de seguros** insurance company
comprar v buy, shop
la compresa sanitary napkin [pad BE]
el comprimido tablet (medicine)
con with; **~ plomo** leaded (gas)
el concierto concert
conducir v drive
conectarse v connect (internet)
la conexión connection (internet); **~ de vuelo** connection (flight)
la conferencia conference
confirmar v confirm
el congelador freezer
la congestión congestion
conocer v meet (someone)
la consigna automática luggage locker
el consulado Consulate

el consultor consultant
contagioso contagious
la contraseña password
el control de pasaportes passport control
el corazón heart
la corbata tie (clothing)
el correo *n* mail (post BE); **~ aéreo** airmail; **~ certificado** registered mail; **~ electrónico** *n* e-mail
cortar *v* cut (hair); **~ en rodajas** to slice
cortarse las puntas *v* trim (hair cut)
el corte *n* cut (injury); **~ de pelo** haircut
corto short
costar *v* cost
la costilla rib (body part)
la crema cream; **~ antiséptica** antiseptic cream; **~ de afeitar** shaving cream; **~ hidratante** lotion
el cristal crystal
el cruce intersection
cuándo when (question)
cuánto cuesta how much
el cubierto utensil
la cuchara spoon; **~ medidora** measuring spoon
la cucharadita teaspoon
la cuchilla desechable disposable razor
el cuchillo knife
el cuello neck; **~ de pico** V-neck; **~ redondo** crew neck
el cuenco bowl
la cuenta account; **~ de ahorro** savings account; **~ corriente** checking (current BE) account
cuero leather
la cueva cave
el cumpleaños birthday
la cuna crib

D

dar to give; **~ el pecho** breastfeed; **~ fuego** light (cigarette); **~ las gracias a** *v* thank
de from, of; **~ acuerdo** OK; **~ la mañana** a.m.; **~ la tarde** p.m.; **~ la zona** local
declarar *v* declare
el dedo finger; **~ del pie** toe
deletrear *v* spell
delicioso delicious
la dentadura denture
el dentista dentist
dentro in
la depilacion wax; **~ de cejas** eyebrow wax; **~ de las ingles** bikini wax
deportes sports
depositar *v* deposit
el depósito bancario deposit (bank)
la derecha right (direction)
desaparecido missing
el desatascador plunger
desatendido unattended
el desayuno breakfast
descansado well-rested
desconectar *v* disconnect (computer)
el descuento discount
desechable disposable
el desierto desert
el desodorante deodorant
despachar medicamentos *v* fill (make up BE) a prescription
el despacho de billetes ticket office
despacio slowly
despertarse *v* wake
después after
el detergente detergent
detrás de behind (direction)
devolver *v* exchange, return (goods)
el día day
diabético diabetic
el diamante diamond
la diarrea diarrhea
el diente tooth
el diesel diesel
difícil difficult
digital digital
el dinero money
la dirección direction
la dirección address; **~ de correo electrónico** e-mail address
discapacitado handicapped [disabled BE]
la discoteca club (dance, night); **~ gay** gay club
disculparse *v* excuse (to get attention)
disfrutar *v* enjoy
disponible available
divorciar *v* divorce
doblada dubbed
doblando (la esquina) around (the corner)
la docena dozen
el documento de identidad identification
el dólar dollar (U.S.)
el dolor pain; **~ de cabeza** headache; **~ de espalda** backache; **~ de estómago** stomachache; **~ de oído** earache; **~ de pecho** chest pain
los dolores menstruales menstrual cramps
dónde where (question)
dormir *v* sleep
el dormitorio dormitory
la ducha shower
dulce sweet (taste)
durante during
el DVD DVD

E

la edad age
el edificio building
el efectivo cash
el efecto secundario side effect
el ejemplar specimen
embarazada pregnant
embarcar v board
la emergencia emergency
el empaste filling (tooth)
empezar v begin, start
empinado steep
empujar v push (door sign)
en la esquina on the corner
el encaje lace
encender v turn on
el enchufe eléctrico electric outlet
encontrarse mal be ill
la enfermedad de transmisión sexual sexually transmitted disease (STD)
el enfermero/la enfermera nurse
enfermo sick
enseñar v show
entender v understand
la entrada admission/cover charge; ~ entrance
entrar v enter
el entretenimiento entertainment
enviar v send, ship; **~ por correo** v mail; **~ un correo electrónico** v e-mail; **~ un fax** v fax; **~ un mensaje de texto** v text (send a message)
envolver v wrap
la época period (of time)
el equipaje luggage [baggage BE]; **~ de mano** carry-on (piece of hand luggage)
el equipo team
el equipo equipment; **~ de buceo** diving equipment; **~ de esnórquel** snorkeling equipment
equis ele (XL) extra large
el error mistake
la erupción cutánea rash
las escaleras stairs; **~ mecánicas** escalators
el escáner scanner
el escaparate window case
la escoba broom
el escozor sting
escribir v write; **~ a máquina** v type
el escurridor colander
el esguince sprain
el esmalte enamel (jewelry)
eso that
España Spain
el español Spanish
la espátula spatula
la especialidad de la casa special (food)
el especialista specialist (doctor)
la espera n wait
esperar v wait
la espuma para el pelo mousse (hair)
el esquí n ski
esquiar v ski
los esquís acuáticos water skis
esta noche tonight
la estaca tent peg
la estación station; **~ de autobuses** bus station; **~ de metro** subway [underground BE] station; **~ de tren** train [railway BE] station
el estadio stadium
el estado de salud condition (medical)
los Estados Unidos United States (U.S.)
estadounidense American
el estanco tobacconist
el estanque pond
estar v be; **~ de paso** v pass through
la estatua statue
el este east
el estilista hairstylist
esto this
el estómago stomach
estrellarse v crash (car)
estreñido constipated
estudiando studying
el estudiante student
estudiar v study
el euro euro
el exceso excess; **~ de velocidad** speeding
la excursión excursion
experto expert (skill level)
la extensión extension (phone)
extraer v extract (tooth)
extraño strange

F

fácil adj easy
la factura bill [invoice BE]
la facturación check-in (airport)
facturar check (luggage)
la falda skirt
la familia family
la farmacia pharmacy [chemist BE]
el fax n fax
la fecha date (calendar)
feliz adj happy
feo adj ugly
el ferry ferry
la fianza deposit (to reserve a room)
la fiebre fever
el film transparente plastic wrap [cling film BE]
el fin de semana weekend
firmar v sign (name)
la flor flower
la fórmula infantil formula (baby)

el formulario form
la foto exposure (film); **~copia** photocopy; **~grafía** photography; **~ digital** digital photo
la fregona mop
los frenos brakes (car)
frente a opposite
fresco fresh
frío *adj* cold (temperature)
las frutas y verduras produce
la frutería y verdulería produce store
el fuego fire
la fuente fountain
fuera outside
el fuerte fort
fumar *v* smoke
la funda para la cámara camera case
el fútbol soccer [football BE]

G

las gafas glasses; **~ de sol** sunglasses
el garaje garage (parking)
la garganta throat
la garrafa carafe
el gas butano cooking gas
la gasolina gas [petrol BE]; **sin plomo** unleaded gas
la gasolinera gas [petrol BE] station
gay gay
el gerente manager
el gimnasio gym

el ginecólogo gynecologist
la gomina gel (hair)
la gota drop (medicine)
grabar *v* burn (CD); **~** *v* engrave
gracias thank you
los grados degrees (temperature); **~ centígrado** Celsius
el gramo gram
grande large
los grandes almacenes department store
la granja farm
gratuito free
gris gray
la grúa tow truck
el grupo group
guapo attractive
guardar *v* save (computer)
la guarnición side dish, order
el guía guide
la guía guide book; **~ de tiendas** store directory
gustar *v* like; **me gusta** I like

H

ha sufrido daños damaged
la habitación room; **~ individual** single room; **~ libre** vacancy
hablar *v* speak
hacer *v* have; **~ una apuesta** *v* place (a bet); **~ un arreglo** *v* alter; **~ una llamada** *v* phone; **~ las maletas** *v* pack; **~ turismo** sightseeing
hambriento hungry
helado icy
la hermana sister
el hermano brother
el hielo ice
el hígado liver (body part)
la hinchazón swelling
hipermétrope farsighted [long-sighted BE]
el hipódromo horsetrack
el hockey hockey; **~ sobre hielo** ice hockey
la hoja de afeitar razor blade
hola hello
el hombre man
el hombro shoulder
hondo deeply
la hora hour
el horario *n* schedule [timetable BE]
los horarios hours; **~ de atención al público** business hours; **~ de oficina** office hours; **~ de visita** visiting hours
las horas de consulta office hours (doctor's)
el hornillo camp stove
el horno stove
el hospital hospital
el hotel hotel

hoy today
el hueso bone

I

el ibuprofeno ibuprofen
la ida y vuelta round-trip [return BE]
la iglesia church
impresionante stunning
imprimir *v* print
el impuesto duty (tax)
incluir *v* include
inconsciente unconscious
increíble amazing
la infección vaginal vaginal infection
infectado infected
el inglés English
iniciar sesión *v* log on (computer)
el insecto bug
la insolación sunstroke
el insomnio insomnia
la insulina insulin
interesante interesting
internacional international (airport area)
la internet internet
el/la intérprete interpreter
el intestino intestine
introducir *v* insert
ir a *v* go (somewhere)
ir de compras *v* go shopping
Irlanda Ireland
irlandés Irish

DICTIONARY

el IVA sales tax [VAT BE]
la izquierda left (direction)

J

el jabón soap
el jardín botánico botanical garden
el jazz jazz
el jersey sweater
joven young
las joyas jewelry
la joyería jeweler
jubilado retired
jugar v play
el juguete toy

K

el kilo kilo; **~gramo** kilogram; **~metraje** mileage
el kilómetro kilometer; **~ cuadrado** square kilometer

L

el labio lip
la laca hairspray
el ladrón thief
el lago lake
la lana wool
la lancha motora motor boat
largo long
el lavabo sink
la lavadora washing machine
la lavandería laundromat [launderette BE]
lavar v wash
el lavavajillas dishwasher
la lección lesson

lejos far
la lengua tongue
la lente lens
las lentillas de contacto contact lens
las letras arts
las libras esterlinas pounds (British sterling)
libre de impuestos duty-free
la librería bookstore
el libro book
la lima de uñas nail file
limpiar v clean
la limpieza de cutis facial
limpio adj clean
la línea line (train)
el lino linen
la linterna flashlight
el líquido liquid; **~ de lentillas de contacto** contact lens solution; **~ lavavajillas** dishwashing liquid
listo ready
la litera berth
el litro liter
la llamada n call; **~ de teléfono** phone call; **~ despertador** wake-up call
llamar v call
la llave key; **~ de habitación** room key; **~ electrónica** key card
el llavero key ring
las llegadas arrivals (airport)
llegar v arrive

llenar v fill
llevar v take; **~ en coche** lift (to give a ride)
la lluvia rain
lluvioso rainy
lo siento sorry
localizar v reach
la luz light (overhead)

M

la madre mother
magnífico magnificent
el malestar estomacal upset stomach
la maleta bag, suitcase
la mandíbula jaw
las mangas cortas short sleeves
las mangas largas long sleeves
la manicura manicure
la mano hand
la manta blanket
mañana tomorrow; **la ~** morning
el mapa map; **~ de carreteras** road map; **~ de ciudad** town map; **~ de la pista** trail [piste BE] map
el mar sea
marcar v dial
mareado dizzy
el mareo motion [travel BE] sickness
el marido husband
marrón brown
el martillo hammer
más more; **~ alto** louder;

~ bajo lower; **~ barato** cheaper; **~ despacio** slower; **~ grande** larger; **~ pequeño** smaller; **~ rápido** faster; **~ tarde** later; **~ temprano** earlier
el masaje massage; **~ deportivo** sports massage
el mástil tent pole
el mecánico mechanic
el mechero lighter
la media hora half hour
mediano medium (size)
la medianoche midnight
el medicamento medicine
el médico doctor
medio half; **~ kilo** half-kilo; **~día** noon [midday BE]
medir v measure (someone)
mejor best
menos less
el mensaje message; **~ instantáneo** instant message
el mercado market
el mes month
la mesa table
el metro subway [underground BE]
el metro cuadrado square meter
la mezquita mosque
el microondas microwave

DICTIONARY

el minibar mini-bar
el minuto minute
el mirador overlook [viewpoint BE] [scenic place]
mirar v look
la misa mass (church service)
mismo same
los mocasines loafers
la mochila backpack
molestar v bother
la moneda coin, currency
mono cute
la montaña n mountain
el monumento conmemorativo memorial (place)
morado purple
el mostrador de información information desk
mostrar v display
la moto acuática jet ski
la motocicleta motorcycle
movilidad mobility
la mujer wife, woman
la multa fine (fee for breaking law)
la muñeca doll; ~ wrist
el músculo muscle
el museo museum
la música music; ~ **clásica** classical music; ~ **folk** folk music; ~ **pop** pop music
el muslo thigh

N

nacional domestic
la nacionalidad nationality
nada nothing
nadar v swim
las nalgas buttocks
naranja orange (color)
la nariz nose
los negocios business
negro black
nevado snowy
la nevera refrigerator
el nieto grandchild
la niña girl
el niño boy, child
el nivel intermedio intermediate
no no
la noche evening, night
el nombre name; ~ **de usuario** username
normal regular
las normas de vestuario dress code
el norte north
la novia girlfriend
el novio boyfriend
el número number; ~ **de fax** fax number; ~ **de permiso de conducir** driver's license number; ~ **de teléfono** phone number; ~ **de teléfono de información** information (phone)

O

la obra de teatro n play (theater)
el oculista optician
el oeste west
la oficina office; ~ **de correos** post office; ~ **de objetos perdidos** lost and found; ~ **de turismo** tourist information office
el ojo eye
la olla pot
la ópera opera
el ordenador computer
la oreja ear
la orina urine
el oro gold; ~ **amarillo** yellow gold; ~ **blanco** white gold
la orquesta orchestra
oscuro dark
el otro camino alternate route
la oxigenoterapia oxygen treatment

P

padecer del corazón heart condition
el padre father
pagar v pay
el pájaro bird
el palacio palace; ~ **de las cortes** parliament building
los palillos chinos chopsticks
la panadería bakery
los pantalones pants [trousers BE]; ~ **cortos** shorts
el pañal diaper [nappy BE]
el pañuelo de papel tissue
el papel paper; ~ **de aluminio** aluminum [kitchen BE] foil; ~ **de cocina** paper towel; ~ **higiénico** toilet paper
el paquete package
para for; ~ **llevar** to go [take away BE]; ~ **no fumadores** non-smoking
el paracetamol acetaminophen [paracetamol BE]
la parada n stop; ~ **de autobús** bus stop
el paraguas umbrella
pararse v stop
el párking parking garage
el parque playpen; ~ park; ~ **de atracciones** amusement park
el partido game; ~ **de fútbol** soccer [football BE] game; ~ **de voleibol** volleyball game
el pasajero passenger; ~ **con billete** ticketed passenger
el pasaporte passport
el pase de acceso a los remontes lift pass
el pasillo aisle
la pasta de dientes toothpaste

la pastelería pastry shop
el patio de recreo playground
el peatón pedestrian
el pecho chest (body part)
el pediatra pediatrician
la pedicura pedicure
pedir v order
el peinado hairstyle
el peine comb
la película movie
peligroso dangerous
el pelo hair
el peltre pewter
la peluquería de caballeros barber
la peluquería hair salon
los pendientes earrings
el pene penis
la penicilina penicillin
la pensión bed and breakfast
pequeño small
perder v lose (something)
perdido lost
el perfume perfume
el periódico newspaper
la perla pearl
permitir v allow, permit
el perro guía guide dog
la persona con discapacidad visual visually impaired person

la picadura de insecto insect bite
picante spicy
picar v stamp (a ticket)
el pie foot
la piel skin
la pierna leg
la pieza part (for car)
los pijamas pajamas
la pila battery
la píldora Pill (birth control)
la piscina pool; ~ **cubierta** indoor pool; ~ **exterior** outdoor pool; ~ **infantil** kiddie [paddling BE] pool
la pista trail [piste BE]
la pizzería pizzeria
el placer pleasure
la plancha n iron (clothes)
planchar v iron
la planta floor [storey BE]; ~ **baja** ground floor
la plata silver; ~ **esterlina** sterling silver
el platino platinum
el plato dish (kitchen); ~ **principal** main course
la playa beach
la plaza town square
la policía police
la pomada cream (ointment)
ponerse en contacto con v contact
por for; ~ **día** per day;

~ **favor** please; ~ **hora** per hour; ~ **la noche** overnight; ~ **noche** per night; ~ **semana** per week
el postre dessert
el precio price
precioso beautiful
el prefijo area code
la pregunta question
presentar v introduce
el preservativo condom
la primera clase first class
primero first
los principales sitios de interés main attraction
principiante beginner, novice (skill level)
la prioridad de paso right of way
la prisa rush
el probador fitting room
probar v taste
el problema problem
el producto good; ~ **de limpieza** cleaning product
programar v schedule
prohibir v prohibit
el pronóstico forecast
pronunciar v pronounce
el protector solar sunscreen
provisional temporary
próximo next
el público public
el pueblo village
el puente bridge

la puerta gate (airport); ~ door; ~ **de incendios** fire door
el pulmón lung
la pulsera bracelet
el puro cigar

Q

qué what (question)
quedar bien v fit (clothing)
quedarse v stay
la queja complaint
la quemadura solar sunburn
querer v love (someone)
quién who (question)
el quiosco newsstand

R

la ración portion; ~ **para niños** children's portion
la rampa para silla de ruedas wheelchair ramp
el rap rap (music)
rápido express, fast
la raqueta racket (sports); ~ **de nieve** snowshoe
la reacción alérgica allergic reaction
recargar v recharge
la recepción reception
la receta prescription
recetar v prescribe
rechazar v decline (credit card)
recibir v receive
el recibo receipt

reciclar recycling
recoger v pick up (something)
la recogida de equipajes baggage claim
la recomendación recommendation
recomendar v recommend
el recorrido tour; **~ en autobús** bus tour; **~ turístico** sightseeing tour
recto straight
el recuerdo souvenir
el regalo gift
la región region
el registro check-in (hotel); **~ del coche** vehicle registration
la regla period (menstrual)
el Reino Unido United Kingdom (U.K.)
la relación relationship
rellenar v fill out (form)
el reloj watch; **~ de pared** wall clock
el remolque trailer
reparar v fix (repair)
el repelente de insectos insect repellent
repetir v repeat
la resaca hangover
la reserva reservation; **~ natural** nature preserve
reservar v reserve
el/la residente de la UE EU resident
respirar v breathe

el restaurante restaurant
retirar v withdraw; **~ fondos** withdrawal (bank)
retrasarse v delay
la reunión meeting
revelar v develop (film)
revisar v check (on something)
la revista magazine
el riñón kidney (body part)
el río river
robado stolen
robar v steal
el robo theft
la rodilla knee
rojo red
romántico romantic
romper v break
la ropa clothing; **~ interior** underwear
rosa pink
roto broken
el rugby rugby
la rueda tire (tyre BE); **~ pinchada** flat tire (tyre BE)
las ruinas ruins
la ruta route; **~ de senderismo** walking route

S

la sábana sheet
el sacacorchos corkscrew
el saco de dormir sleeping bag
la sala room; **~ de conciertos** concert hall; **~ de espera** waiting room; **~ de reuniones** meeting room
la salida check-out (hotel)
la salida n exit; **~ de urgencia** emergency exit
las salidas departures (airport)
salir v exit, leave
el salón room; **~ de congresos** convention hall; **~ de juegos recreativos** arcade; **~ de manicura** nail salon
¡Salud! Cheers!
la salud health
las sandalias sandals
sangrar v bleed
la sangre blood
el santuario shrine
la sartén frying pan
la sauna sauna
el secador de pelo hair dryer
la secreción discharge (bodily fluid)
la seda silk
sediento thirsty
la seguridad security
el seguro insurance
seguro safe (protected)
el sello n stamp (postage)
el semáforo traffic light
la semana week
semanal weekly
el seminario seminar
el sendero trail; **~ para bicicletas** bike route
el seno breast
sentarse v sit
separado separated (marriage)
ser v be
serio serious
el servicio restroom (toilet BE); **~ service** (in a restaurant); **~ completo** full-service; **~ de habitaciones** room service; **~ inalámbrico a internet** wireless internet service; **~ de internet** internet service; **~ de lavandería** laundry service; **~ de limpieza de habitaciones** housekeeping service
la servilleta napkin
sí yes
el sida AIDS
la silla chair; **~ para niños** child seat; **~ de ruedas** wheelchair
el símbolo symbol (keyboard)
sin without; **~ alcohol** non-alcoholic; **~ grasa** fat free; **~ receta** over the counter (medication)
la sinagoga synagogue
el sitio de interés attraction (place)
el sobre envelope

el socorrista lifeguard
el sol sun
solamente only
soleado sunny
solo alone
soltero single (marriage)
el sombrero hat
la somnolencia drowsiness
sordo deaf
soso bland
el suavizante conditioner
el subtítulo subtitle
sucio dirty
la sudadera sweatshirt
el suelo floor
el sujetador bra
súper super (fuel)
superior upper
el supermercado grocery store, supermarket
la supervisión supervision
el sur south
el surfista windsurfer

T

la tabla board; ~ **de snowboard** snowboard; ~ **de surf** surfboard
la talla size; ~ **grande** plus size; ~ **pequeña** petite size
el taller garage (repair)
el talón de equipaje luggage [baggage BE] ticket
el tampón tampon
la taquilla locker; ~ reservation desk
tarde late (time)
la tarde afternoon
la tarjeta card; ~ **de cajero automático** ATM card; ~ **de crédito** credit card; ~ **de débito** debit card; ~ **de embarque** boarding pass; ~ **internacional de estudiante** international student card; ~ **de memoria** memory card; ~ **de negocios** business card; ~ **postal** postcard; ~ **de seguro** insurance card; ~ **de socio** membership card; ~ **telefónica** phone card
la tasa fee
el taxi taxi
la taza cup; ~ **medidora** measuring cup
el teatro theater; ~ **de la ópera** opera house
la tela impermeable groundcloth [groundsheet BE]
el teleférico cable car
el teléfono telephone; ~ **móvil** cell [mobile BE] phone; ~ **público** pay phone
la telesilla chair lift
el telesquí ski/drag lift
la televisión TV
el templo temple (religious)
temprano early
el tenedor fork
tener v have; ~ **dolor** v hurt (have pain); ~ **náuseas** v be nauseous
el tenis tennis
la tensión arterial blood pressure
la terminal terminal (airport)
terminar v end
la terracotta terracotta
terrible terrible
el texto n text (message)
el tiempo time; ~ weather
la tienda store; ~ **de alimentos naturales** health food store; ~ **de antigüedades** antique store; ~ **de bebidas alcohólicas** liquor store [off-licence BE]; ~ **de campaña** tent; ~ **de deportes** sporting goods store; ~ **de fotografía** camera store; ~ **de juguetes** toy store; ~ **de música** music store; ~ **de recuerdos** souvenir store; ~ **de regalos** gift shop; ~ **de ropa** clothing store
las tijeras scissors
la tintorería dry cleaner
el tipo de cambio exchange rate
tirar v pull (door sign)
la tirita bandage
la toalla towel
la toallita baby wipe
el tobillo ankle
el torneo de golf golf tournament
la torre tower
la tos n cough
toser v cough
el total total (amount)
trabajar v work
tradicional traditional
traducir v translate
traer v bring
tragar v swallow
el traje suit
tranquilo quiet
el tren train; ~ **rápido** express train
triste sad
la trona highchair
el trozo piece
la tumbona deck chair
el turista tourist

U

último last
la universidad university
uno one
la uña nail; ~ **del dedo** fingernail; ~ **del pie** toenail
urgente urgent
usar v use

DICTIONARY

V

las vacaciones vacation [holiday BE]
vaciar v empty
la vacuna vaccination
la vagina vagina
la validez valid
valioso valuable
el valle valley
el valor value
el vaquero denim
los vaqueros jeans
el viaje trip
el vaso glass (drinking)
el váter químico chemical toilet
vegetariano vegetarian
la vejiga bladder
vender v sell
el veneno poison
venir v come
la ventana window
el ventilador fan (appliance)
ver v see
verde green
el vestido dress (piece of clothing)
el viaje trip
el vidrio glass (material)
viejo old
la viña vineyard
la violación n rape
violar v rape
el visado visa (passport document)
visitar v visit
la vitamina vitamin
la vitrina display case
viudo widowed
vivir v live
vomitar v vomit **el vuelo** flight; **~ internacional** international flight; **~ nacional** domestic flight

Z

la zapatería shoe store
las zapatillas slippers; **~ de deporte** sneaker
los zapatos shoes
la zona area; **~ de compras** shopping area; **~ de fumadores** smoking area; **~ para picnic** picnic area
el zoológico zoo
zurcir v mend

INDEX

Accommodation 115
activities for children 95
adventure sports 92
airports 116

Bahía Solano 80
Barichara 40
    Catedral de la Inmaculada Concepción 40
    Jardin 41
    Parque Principal 40
Barranquilla 53
    Catedral San Nicolas de Tolentino 54
    Museo del Caribe 54
    Museo Romantico 54
    Paseo Bolívar 54
    Plaza San Nicolas 53
    Terminal de Transportes Metropolitano 53
Bocagrande 51
Bogotá
    Alcaldia 26
    Cerro Monserrate 28
    El Catedral 26
    El Chapinero 29
    Iglesia de Nuestra Señora de Egipto 26
    La Candelaria 25
    LGBT community center 29
    Mercado de Paloquemao 28
    Museo Botero 26
    Museo de la Independencia 27
    Museo del Oro 27
    Palacio de Justicia 26
    Parque Periodista 25
    Parque Santander 27
    Plaza Bolívar 26
    Plaza del Chorro de Quevedo 26
    Zona Rosa 29
budgeting 116
Bucaramanga 41
    Casa de Bolívar 42
    Catedral de la Sagrada Familia 42
    Iglesia San Pio 42
    Museo de Arte Moderno 42
    Parque García Rovira 41
    Parque San Pio 42
    Parque Santander 42

Cabo de la Vela 62
Caño Cristales 81
Cali 68
car rental 117
Cartagena 48
    Baluarte San Francisco Javier 49
    Calle del Arsenal 49
    Casa de Gabriel García Márquez 51
    Casa del Marqués del Premio Real 48, 50
    Convento San Francisco 49
    Convento Santa Teresa 50
    Convento Santo Domingo 51
    El Bodegón de la Candelaria 50
    Iglesia de Santísma Trinidad 49
    Iglesia Santo Toribio de Mogrovejo 51
    La India Catalina 49
    Museo de Arte Moderno 50
    Palacio de la Inquisición 50
    Palacio de la Proclamación 50
    Palacio Municipal 50
    Playa Barahona 49
    Plaza de Bolívar 50
    Plaza de la Aduana 49
    Plaza de los Coches 49
    Plaza San Pedro 50
    Plaza Santo Domingo 51
    Puente Román 49
    San Pedro Claver 50
Chicamocha Canyon 39
Chocó 75
Ciudad Perdida 58
Cúcuta 42
    Casa de la Cultura 43
    Catedral de San José 43
crime and safety 118
customs 119
Disabled travelers 119

El Cable 45
El Peñol 35
El Pueblito 58
El Valle 79
electricity 120
embassies and consulates 120

INDEX

emergency numbers 120

Festivals 96

Guajira 59
Guatapé 34
　El Peñol 35

Hacienda Napoles 37
health and medical care 122

Ipiales 74
Isla de Barú 52
Isla de Los Micos 84
Isla Tierrabomba 52

Jardín 36
　Principle Park 36
　Templo de la Inmaculada Concepción 36

Leticia 81
LGBTQ travelers 124

Maicao 64
Manizales 44
　Cathedral Basílica Metropolitana de Nuestra Señora del Rosario 45
　El Cable 45
　La Gobernación 44
　Parque Chipre 45
　Plaza de Bolívar 44
Medellín 32
　Catedral Metropolitano 33
　El Poblado 34
　Iglesia de la Veracruz 33
　Iglesia de San José 34
　Joaquin Antonio Uribe Botanical Garden 34
　Mercado de San Alejo 33
　Museo de Antioquia 33
　Palacio de la Cultura Rafael Uribe 33
　Parque Bolívar 33
　Parque de Berrio 33
　Parque Lleras 34
　Parque San Antonio 33
　Plaza Botero 32
Monumento Las Tres Cruces 71
money 125

Nightlife 125
Nuquí 78

Opening hours 126
Orchideorama 71

Palomino 60
Paraguachón 64
Parque Ecológico Río Blanco 45
Parque Nacional Los Nevados 47
Parque Nacional Natural Macuira 63
Parque Nacional Natural Tayrona 57
Parque Nacional Natural Utria 79
Parque Nacional Natural Utría 78
Pereira 46
　Plaza de Bolívar 46
Playa Blanca 52
Popayán 71
Providencia 67
public holiday 126
Puerto Nariño 84
Punta Gallinas 62

Quibdó 77

Religious services 127
Reserva Natural Cañon del Río Claro 37
Riohacha 59
Rodadero 56

Salento 47
Nuestra Señora del Carmen 47
San Andrés 65
San Antonio 70
San Gil 38
　Catedral de la Santa Cruz 39
　Central Comercial El Puente 39
　Parque Gallineral 39
　Parque Principal 39
Santa Fe de Antioquia 35
　Catedral Basilica de la Inmaculada Concepción de Santa Fe 35
　Plaza Mayor 35
Santa Marta 54
　Catedral Basílica de Santa Marta 55
　Casa de la Aduana 55
　La Herencia Tairona 54
　Museo del Oro 55
　Plaza Bolívar 55
Santuario de Fauna y Flora Los Flamencos 60
shopping 87
smoking 128

Taganga 56
tax 128
telephones 128
Tierradentro 73
tour operators 130
transport 130

Uribía 61

Villa de Leyva 30
  Iglesia de Nuestra Señora del Rosario 30
  Plaza Mayor 30

visas 132

Women travelers 133

Zipaquirá 30
  Cathedral de Sal 30

Berlitz pocket guide

COLOMBIA

First Edition 2019

Editor: Tom Fleming
Author: Chris Wallace
Head of DTP and Pre-Press: Rebeka Davies
Picture Editor: Tom Smyth
Cartography Update: Carte
Photography Credits: Alamy 69, 76, 86, 99, 100; AWL Images 1, 52; Getty Images 5TC, 13, 43, 44, 78, 80; Granger/REX/Shutterstock 17; iStock 4MC, 4TL, 5T, 5MC, 6R, 7, 24, 29, 31, 48, 51, 55, 58, 70, 89; PA Images 21; Robert Harding 39; Sebastian Sanint/ProColombia 4TC; Shutterstock 4ML, 5M, 5MC, 5M, 6L, 7R, 14, 18, 27, 32, 35, 36, 41, 46, 57, 61, 63, 67, 73, 75, 83, 85, 90, 93, 94, 103; SuperStock 11, 64
Cover Picture: SuperStock

Distribution
UK, Ireland and Europe: Apa Publications (UK) Ltd; sales@insightguides.com
United States and Canada: Ingram Publisher Services; ips@ingramcontent.com
Australia and New Zealand: Woodslane; info@woodslane.com.au
Southeast Asia: Apa Publications (SN) Pte; singaporeoffice@insightguides.com
Worldwide: Apa Publications (UK) Ltd; sales@insightguides.com

Special Sales, Content Licensing and CoPublishing
Insight Guides can be purchased in bulk quantities at discounted prices. We can create special editions, personalised jackets and corporate imprints tailored to your needs. sales@insightguides.com; www.insightguides.biz

All Rights Reserved
© 2019 Apa Digital (CH) AG and Apa Publications (UK) Ltd

Printed in China by CTPS

No part of this book may be reproduced, stored in a retrieval system or transmitted in any form or means electronic, mechanical, photocopying, recording or otherwise, without prior written permission from Apa Publications.

Contact us
Every effort has been made to provide accurate information in this publication, but changes are inevitable. The publisher cannot be responsible for any resulting loss, inconvenience or injury. We would appreciate it if readers would call our attention to any errors or outdated information. We also welcome your suggestions; please contact us at: berlitz@apaguide.co.uk
www.insightguides.com/berlitz

Berlitz Trademark Reg. U.S. Patent Office and other countries. Marca Registrada. Used under licence from the Berlitz Investment Corporation

Berlitz®

speaking your language

phrase book & dictionary
phrase book & CD

Available in: Arabic, Brazilian Portuguese*, Burmese*, Cantonese Chinese, Croatian, Czech*, Danish*, Dutch, English, Filipino, Finnish*, French, German, Greek, Hebrew*, Hindi*, Hungarian*, Indonesian, Italian, Japanese, Korean, Latin American Spanish, Malay, Mandarin Chinese, Mexican Spanish, Norwegian, Polish, Portuguese, Romanian*, Russian, Spanish, Swedish, Thai, Turkish, Vietnamese
*Book only

www.berlitzpublishing.com